MSP® Survival Guide for Business Change Managers

London: TSO

information & publishing solutions

Published by TSO (The Stationery Office) and available from:

Online
www.tsoshop.co.uk

Mail, Telephone, Fax & E-mail
TSO
PO Box 29, Norwich, NR3 1GN
Telephone orders/General enquiries: 0870 600 5522
Fax orders: 0870 600 5533
E-mail: customer.services@tso.co.uk
Textphone: 0870 240 3701

TSO@Blackwell and other Accredited Agents

A CIP catalogue record for this book is available from the British Library

A Library of Congress CIP catalogue record has been applied for.

First published 2014

ISBN 9780113314461

Printed in the United Kingdom for The Stationery Office
Material is FSC certified. Sourced from responsible sources.
P002627434 c5 08/14

Contents

List of figures

List of tables

Acknowledgements

ABOUT THE AUTHOR

Rod Sowden of Aspire Europe Ltd is the author of *Managing Successful Programmes* (MSP®) and co-author of the latest version of P3M3®.

He founded Aspire Europe in 2004, which is dedicated to improving organizations' transformational programme performance. The guidance in this publication has been drawn from a wide range of sectors and experience gained over many years of authoring and supporting improved programme management. More information on Aspire Europe can be found at www.aspireeurope.com

AUTHOR ACKNOWLEDGEMENTS

The author would like to express his grateful thanks for the support and contributions of Tom Ford, Claire Rookes, Alice Sowden and Alan Summerfield (all team members of Aspire Europe).

He would also like to acknowledge other close associates for their ideas and motivation, notably David Trussler (Transformation Director, Plymouth CC) and Andy Murray (Director, Outperform Ltd and lead author for PRINCE2009 and P3M3 2014).

PUBLISHER ACKNOWLEDGEMENTS

TSO would like to thank the following people for generously donating their time to reviewing this publication: Mike Acaster, AXELOS; Grant Avery, Outcome Insights, New Zealand; Robert Cole, the Centre for Change Management; Andy Goodchild, Devon and Somerset Fire and Rescue Service; Geof Leigh, Goaldart Ltd; and Liz Pattison, Transport Systems Catapult.

PART 1
Introduction to programme management

The survival guide

1

1   The survival guide

You have just left the chief's office and are in a bit of a quandary. You had heard about the organization adopting programme management, and you even knew it was based on something called 'MSP', but you hadn't expected to be involved as it was project stuff that did not really affect you.

You have just been asked to take on the role of business change manager (BCM) for one of the programmes. The inference is that it is a career-enhancing move, but as you have been doing well anyway you aren't too sure if you need this kind of risk in your career plan.

You have been told that it is a critical role in delivering the strategic change but the chief seemed a bit light on detail about what it involved, and no one else has been offered this opportunity in the organization before so you will be breaking new ground. This seems to be an opportunity to enhance or threaten your good track record.

You have decided to find out more about the role and promised to get back to the chief with your decision. If this sounds familiar, this is the publication for you.

Managing Successful Programmes or MSP® (Cabinet Office, 2011) is a guide which captures a body of knowledge around the complex topic of programme management. It is regarded as the definitive guide and is written for a very wide audience indeed. It has grown significantly in the last 10 years as knowledge of the topic has increased, but it cannot cater for specific needs of individuals and sectors.

This survival guide has been written for people who have one of the core roles in a programme. It provides specific, practical advice on how to be effective in a way that the more formal main guide cannot.

The publication extracts the core text from MSP that is important in explaining a key concept, so it provides the main facts from the guide while applying these concepts to scenarios which will help you understand the concepts.

This publication is intended to be your reference guide, your mentor and the basis to help you perform your role to the best of your ability.

'I am neither frustrated nor planning anything other than being the best Secretary of State I could be.' Hillary Clinton

That is a pretty good ambition for you as a BCM too, so on that note, it's time to send the chief an email and say that you welcome the challenge!

Introducing *Managing Successful Programmes*

2

2 Introducing *Managing Successful Programmes*

This chapter provides you with a summary of the key concepts from *Managing Successful Programmes* (MSP) so that you are familiar with the terminology. It can also act as a quick reference for some of the key concepts that you will need to consider at the outset.

MSP isn't the only programme management framework. There is also an approach from an organization called the Project Management Institute (PMI), but it tends to focus on capital programmes such as information technology, engineering and construction. If your programme comes into any of these categories, it would be worth investigating PMI as it has some excellent content.

2.1 WHAT IS PROGRAMME MANAGEMENT?

MSP defines programme management as 'the action of carrying out the coordinated organization, direction and implementation of a dossier of projects and transformational activities (i.e. the programme) to achieve outcomes and realize benefits of strategic importance to the business'.

A simpler definition is that 'programme management is the delivery of structural change'. This is valid for a single organization, multiple organizations, market or social transformation. Programme management will deliver structural change and the business change manager (BCM) role is all about making that happen.

Programme management aligns three critical organizational elements (Figure 2.1):

- Corporate strategy
- Delivery mechanisms for change (projects)
- Business as usual and operations environment.

It manages the natural tension that exists between these elements to deliver transformational change that meets the needs of the organization and its stakeholders.

Programmes can deliver the means to allow business operations to change, but they do not run business operations. It is the senior operational managers,

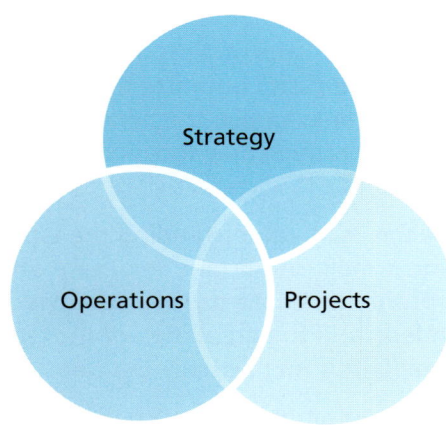

Figure 2.1 Organizational elements of programme management

not the programme, who will have to make the changed operations work better than before to realize the benefits for the long term.

In a programme there are three core roles on the programme board. The corporate strategy is represented by the senior responsible owner (SRO), while the delivery of the new capability mainly from projects is the responsibility of the programme manager. The definition of the business capability, maintenance of the operational performance and subsequent delivery of benefits is the responsibility of the BCM.

This is why you as BCM must have detailed understanding of the business operations and the respect of the operational teams as you will be leading them through turbulent times and delivering change.

2.2 TYPES OF PROGRAMME

There are three distinct types of programme defined in the MSP guide. These are described in Table 2.1.

In reality, most programmes have a mix of these characteristics, but it is helpful to understand the dominant characteristics of a programme as it will help to develop and optimize the priorities and approach. For example, the benefits for a compliance programme may focus on the avoidance of penalties.

For you, as the BCM, understanding the type of programme is really important. It is quite often the case that programmes are trumpeted as visionary (i.e. vision-led), and the great idea of the chief, when in reality this isn't actually the case.

Compliance programmes are much more common than is normally recognized. This is because there is a tendency to disguise them as vision-led, which

creates more excitement. It is common for change to be forced on the organization by external events. There is no choice, and whether the organization spotted that change early and was first to move, or was last because everyone else already had, is just a matter of timing. Disguising a compliance programme as a vision-led programme can be fraught with danger.

Some examples

A large bank had a vision-led programme to change its foreign currency trading systems. The programme was certainly big, complex and expensive, but after some investigation it transpired that the existing systems were so outdated that they were losing a significant market share. Therefore, the programme was more compliance than vision-led as the only other real option was to withdraw from currency trading, which wasn't acceptable. The main competitors already had similar systems in place.

A new director general at a large UK public sector organization outlined a vision for the corporation, with 20% fewer staff, and leaner and more efficient operations. The organization was already lean and efficient so the vision didn't stand up to scrutiny or dialogue. The reality was that it was another compliance programme as the organization was having central budget cuts imposed on it by government, so it had to comply.

It is very rare to find a genuinely 'blue sky' vision-led programme where there are no precedents or work going on in the organization. There may be situations where previous work is swept aside by the energy of a new programme, but it is wise not to throw out good work. Consequently, the

Table 2.1 MSP programme types

Programme type	Characteristics
Vision-led	Has come into existence to deliver a clearly defined vision that has been created and is sponsored by the top of the organization
	Tends to be top down in approach, with cross-functional implications for the organization's operations
	Entrepreneurial programmes developing new products and services, that focus on innovation or strategic opportunity offered by the business environment
	In the public sector, this could be the translation of political priorities into a programme which will refine and deliver the desired changes
Emergent	Evolves from concurrent, individual projects that have grown within an organization. There is now recognition that coordination of the projects is necessary to deliver the changes and the desired benefits
	Is transitory, as it becomes a planned programme when its vision, context and direction have been defined and established
Compliance	May also be referred to as a 'must do' programme
	The organization has no choice but to change as a result of an external event, such as legislative change
	Benefits may be expressed in terms of compliance, achievement and avoidance of negative implications rather than measurable improvements in performance

start of many programmes is actually to review what is going on and what can be used in the new initiative.

Whatever type of programme it is, you will be delivering fundamental change of some sort, so you should make sure you are clear about what the drivers for that change are and the source of the energy, as you will need to harness and direct it. If the source of the energy is misunderstood, then you will lose momentum.

2.3 IMPACTS OF PROGRAMMES

Each type of programme reflects its energy source and the impacts will also vary. Table 2.2 shows the characteristics or different programme impacts as described in MSP.

The impact of the programmes will vary from sector to sector. Private sector programmes are likely to deliver some sort of specific infrastructure capability, affect internal structure or be trying to affect change in a market or market position. Public sector programmes will do the same but may be trying to affect changes in society and the economy rather than gain market advantage.

Table 2.2 Impacts of programme types

Programme impact	Characteristics
Specification-led	Where the change being delivered is based on the making and delivering of new facilities, the programme will tend to be led by the specification of the outputs required – for example, a major capital construction programme. There will be relatively low levels of ambiguity about what the programme is to deliver but there may be high levels of complexity and risk in the delivery. The scope will be reasonably well defined and adjusted according to circumstances. MSP's approach can be used in this type of programme but may need to be scaled down, as some of its elements may not be required.
Business transformation	Where the change is more focused on transforming the way the organization functions (for example, implementing a new service partnership or moving into a new market) the programme will tend to be vision-led with desired outcomes and associated benefits. There is likely to be ambiguity about the overall implication of the changes; for instance, it may not be known how some parts of the organization will react. The greater the impact on customers and the markets, the greater the levels of ambiguity and risk.
Political and societal	Where the change is focused on improvements in society, the level of predictability will be reduced, as there will be many uncontrollable external factors also at play. For example, a change that aims to improve the early education of pre-school-age children in order to increase their likelihood of making a more meaningful contribution to society when they leave full-time education will not only take time to design and introduce but the implications for the students and the economy will not necessarily be controllable or predictable in the long term. The scope may need to be adjusted as ambiguities are clarified and the changes are delivered in steps (tranches) over a number of years. MSP is highly suitable for programmes with a high level of complexity, ambiguity and risk. The programme management framework of MSP is primarily designed to cater for leading and managing transformational change.

The three impacts are equally relevant to both types of organization. One thing that is for sure is that a programme will deliver some sort of major structural change that will have a lasting effect.

Table 2.3 gives some examples.

Not all programmes are quite so spectacular as some of those listed in Table 2.3, but hopefully the table will help illustrate that programme management is not applicable to only one sector and that these 'impacts' apply to all but sometimes need a bit of thought.

As with the 'types', most programmes will actually have multiple 'impacts' as well. This is important for the BCM as it will affect the scope and scale of the programme and the effect on the operational areas that you are responsible for. The building of a high speed rail link is a complex engineering challenge that could be achieved by a large project, but generation of economic activity along the

Table 2.3 Programme impact examples

Impact	Private sector	Public sector
Specification-led	New distribution network, warehouses, vehicles, ICT etc. (e.g. for a supermarket distributor)	Major new power generation (e.g. Three Gorges Dam project in China)
	New oil exploration platforms (e.g. deep sea)	New transport infrastructure (e.g. the High Speed 2 (HS2) rail link in the UK)
Business transformation	Merger or acquisition of two large organizations (e.g. UK banks)	Service partner model (e.g. health care provision)
	Adoption of a major new technology (e.g. an enterprise-wide technology)	Deregulation of a sector or market (e.g. banking)
Political and societal	Change market behaviours (e.g. mobile applications)	Change the way a market works (e.g. use of non-carbon fuels)
	Create new customer interfaces and channels (e.g. online purchasing)	Reduction in obesity or smoking

route will be needed to justify the investment (business transformation) and there will need to be preparation to change societal behaviours to take advantage of this new capability for travel.

Similarly, a private sector organization that invests heavily in a new logistics infrastructure will expect benefits to be managed, which could involve process changes, organizational structure changes and cultural acceptance of a changed approach.

The BCM is likely to be heavily involved with delivering the business transformation and political/societal aspects of a programme, as these are where the benefits will be generated, so the BCM role is all about delivering change and releasing benefits.

Figure 2.2 is critical to understanding the difference between the programme manager and BCM roles. The boxes on the left show what the programme manager delivers while the boxes on the right show what you (the BCM) deliver. As you can see, the roles

are fundamentally different in their focus. Once the programme manager has delivered the outputs and created the capability, the BCM takes that forward to deliver the outcomes and benefits.

Programmes normally serve to deliver corporate objectives, as shown in the list below:

- The corporate objectives drive the development of the programme vision.
- The vision is expanded into a blueprint for the future organization.
- The blueprint defines what the projects need to create.
- The projects deliver outputs, which create capabilities.
- The capabilities are transitioned into outcomes.
- The outcomes enable the realization of benefits.
- The benefits are then achieved and contribute to the achievement of the corporate objectives.

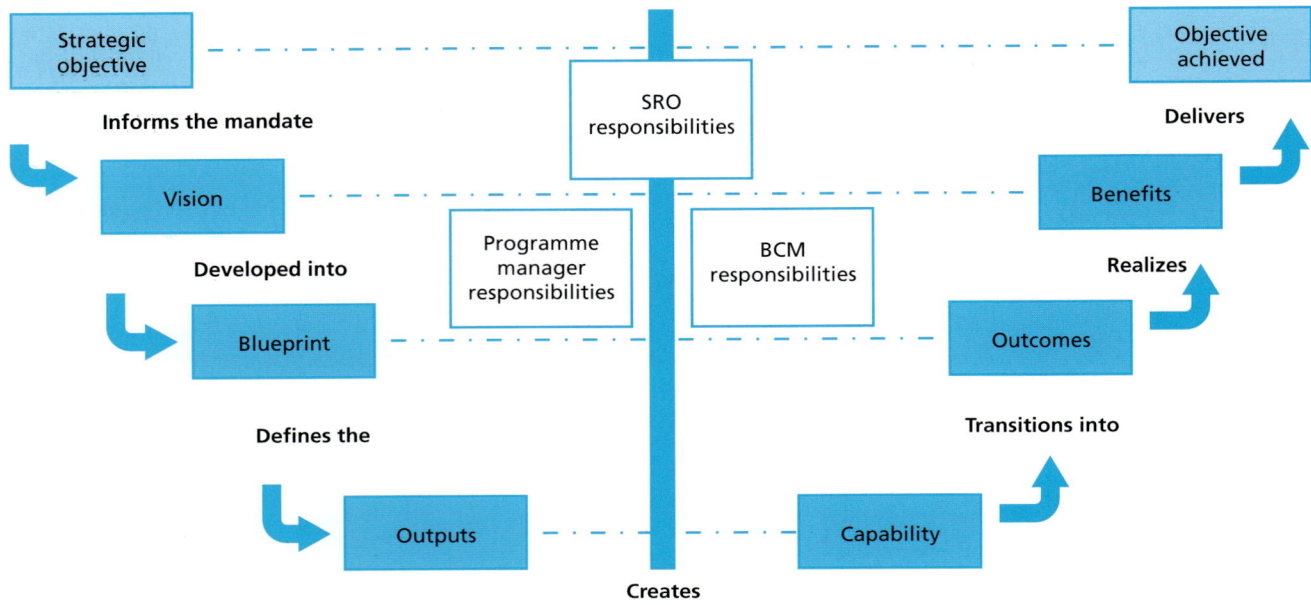

Figure 2.2 Programme delivery responsibilities

2.4 HAVE YOU ACTUALLY GOT A PROGRAMME?

There is often a bit of a problem with the 'P' word. This is because organizations fail to actually define what it means to them. There are three main concepts that lurk around the P word:

- Portfolio
- Programmes
- Projects.

They are distinct and quite different from each other, but there are also a number of similarities.

The standard definitions from the AXELOS common glossary are:

- A **portfolio** is the totality of an organization's investment (or segment thereof) in the changes required to achieve its strategic objectives, and portfolio management is a coordinated collection of strategic processes and decisions that together enable the most effective balance of organizational change and business as usual/operations. If your programme has no end date or looks to be continual, you may well have a portfolio.

- A **programme** is defined as a temporary, flexible organization created to coordinate, direct and oversee the implementation of a set of related projects and activities in order to deliver outcomes and benefits related to the organization's strategic objectives. A programme is likely to have a life that spans several years. Programmes deal with outcomes; projects deal with outputs.

- A **project** is also a temporary organization, usually existing for a much shorter duration, which will deliver one or more outputs in accordance with an agreed business case. A particular project may or may not be part of a programme.

Programme management and project management are complementary approaches rather than alternatives, which is sometimes the interpretation. During a programme lifecycle, projects are initiated, run and closed. Programmes provide an umbrella under which these projects can be coordinated.

There is also a really useful framework called the Portfolio, Programme and Project Management Maturity Model (P3M3®), which is a model for assessing the maturity of the organization. P3M3 uses a number of perspectives that are common to all three disciplines, namely:

- Organizational governance
- Management control
- Benefits management
- Risk management
- Stakeholder management
- Finance management
- Resource management.

As can be seen, there are a lot of areas that are common, and it is easy to make the wrong choice without appropriate experience.

P3M3 deals with analysing the maturity of organizations and the characteristics that affect this. The fact that your organization is appointing BCMs is a sign of increasing maturity, and the P3M3 framework provides a very useful set of checklists for the way your organization manages programmes.

A maturity assessment of your organization, using P3M3, would be very valuable for you; the lower the maturity, the lower the formality and support that will be available to you as a BCM, which increases your personal risk exposure.

So, what does all that mean to you as the BCM? Well it means you need to be careful about what it is you are being asked to contribute to and it will affect how effective you can be in your role.

It is quite common for the word 'programme' to be used to describe things that aren't programmes, so you might like to look through the following checklist of things that can cause confusion:

- Has it got a start and end or is it continual? If it is seen as continual, then it is more likely to be a portfolio.
- Is the term 'programme of work' used? If so, it is more likely to be an ongoing investment in refurbishment or maintenance.
- Is it scoped to deliver transformational change? If not, then it is more likely to be a project and the BCM is actually the customer for the products.
- Is it being driven by the need to change or the need to build something? If it is the latter then it will be more likely to operate like a project.

Projects that are delivering some form of structural change will struggle with traditional forms of project management, which evolved from engineering, construction and ICT. The techniques in MSP can really help these types of project, as a programme is more adaptable to change and the techniques are more agile.

2.5 WHAT IS MSP?

As much of the guidance in this publication is based on the MSP framework, it is helpful to understand

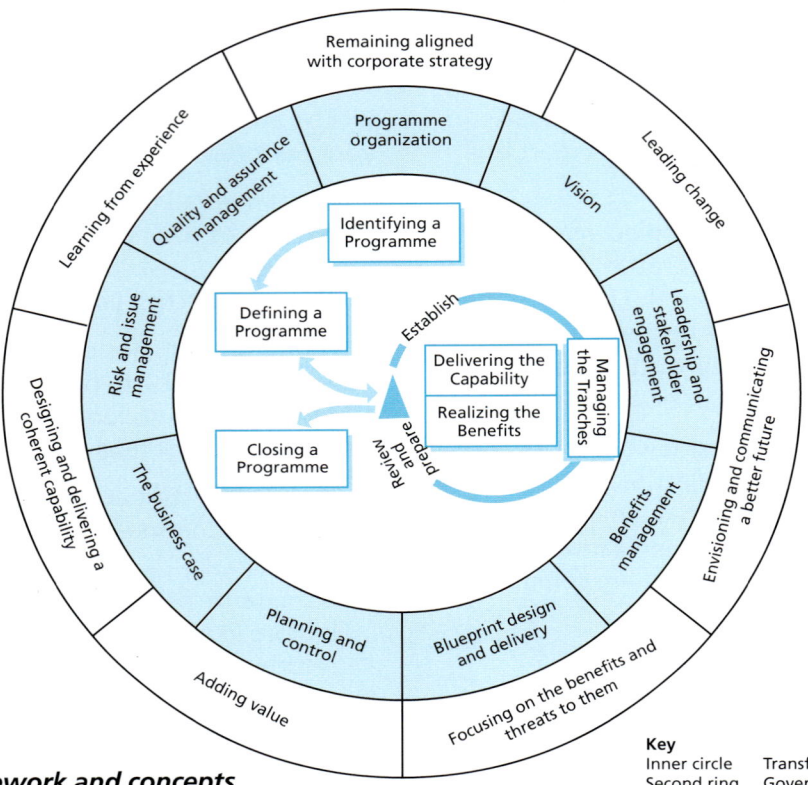

Figure 2.3 MSP framework and concepts

Key
Inner circle — Transformational flow
Second ring — Governance themes
Outer ring — Principles

the basic ideas. MSP is made up of principles, themes and a lifecycle called the transformational flow (see Figure 2.3).

Before describing the basic MSP framework, it is important for the BCM and other roles to appreciate that MSP has been developed to meet a range of requirements and sectors.[1] In most organizations, the MSP framework needs to be adapted to a more definitive method suited to the organizational context and the specific needs of individual

programmes (while still maintaining consistency wherever possible). A good way of adapting MSP would be to integrate the lifecycle with the roles and the themes.

The following sections give a quick summary of what the framework contains.

2.5.1 The principles

The principles are self-validating, universal and empowering. They apply to all aspects of the delivery of the programme:

---

1 In this context, a sector is reflecting a wider change than within an organization (e.g. a market, region, community, economy, social group or other grouping that may be affected by a change programme).

- **Remaining aligned with corporate strategy** A programme is typically a large investment that should make a significant contribution towards achieving corporate performance targets. A well-managed programme maintains good links with a sometimes volatile corporate strategy.
- **Leading change** Seeing through change in a programme is a leadership challenge. In addition to the need to manage a large number of complex tasks, people need to be led. It is impossible to move to a better future without clear leadership.
- **Envisioning and communicating a better future** A programme is relevant where there is a need to achieve transformational change, where there is some marked step change or break with the present required in the future capability. In order to achieve such a beneficial, future state, the leaders of a programme must first describe a clear vision of that future.
- **Focusing on the benefits and threats to them** Best-practice programme management aligns everything towards satisfying strategic objectives by realizing the end benefits. Thus the programme's boundary, including the projects and activities that become part of the programme, are determined to enable the realization of these end benefits. The ultimate success of a programme is judged by its ability to realize these benefits and their continuing relevance to the strategic context. If the benefits are of strategic value, then effective risk management is crucial.
- **Adding value** A programme only remains valid if it adds value to the sum of its constituent projects and major activities. If it is found to add nothing then it is better to close the programme and allow the projects to proceed independently coordinated by corporate portfolio management.

- **Designing and delivering a coherent capability** The programme will deliver a business architecture or final capability. This should have such internal coherence that all quality requirements are optimized, being released into operational use according to a schedule delivering maximum incremental capability with minimal adverse operational impact.
- **Learning from experience** A programme is a learning organization in that it reflects upon and improves its own performance during its life. Good governance requires approaches to managing the different themes that are regularly adjusted and adapted on the basis of experience and results so far. For example, part of good benefits realization management means that stakeholders are identifying new opportunities to realize benefits as their awareness and experience increase.

2.5.2 Governance themes

The themes are a set of references that explain how key elements of the programme should be delivered during its delivery lifecycle. The governance themes cover subjects that will need to be constantly managed to a greater or lesser extent on a daily basis:

- **Programme organization** describes how governance should be applied, through the sponsoring group and programme board, and provides guidance on the roles and responsibilities for the senior responsible owner, business change manager and programme manager. It also recommends additional roles.
- **Vision** is required for the delivery of any programme; MSP sets out the key contents and how it should paint a picture of a better future for the organization.

- **Leadership and stakeholder engagement** is critical to any programme because change requires effective leadership. MSP emphasizes the need to identify and communicate with stakeholders and provides analysis tools to generate greater understanding of their needs, perceptions and priorities.
- **Benefits management** is the core difference between projects and programmes. The active exploitation of the opportunities that are offered by the investment in projects' deliverables is complex, with each benefit having its own profile and a supporting plan to deliver the changes and release the dividend.
- **Blueprint design and delivery** form the foundation for the programme; what is the 'to-be' state for the organization when the programme completes, and in fact what is our starting point ('as-is' state)? Transformation is delivered in step changes through tranches.
- **Planning and control** are covered in detail to explain how to develop the programme plan and maintain internal control of the projects to ensure that the programme remains on course.
- **The business case** will be in place for all programmes, with MSP highlighting the need for the programme to have an overarching case, and each project having its own business case too.
- **Risk and issue management** offers advice and guidance on how to avoid the realization of the events that will cause the programme to fail. It focuses on the need not only to manage threats, but also to exploit opportunities. There are four perspectives: strategic, programme, operation and project risk.
- **Quality and assurance management** describes how there should be optimal management of people, resources, suppliers, processes, assets, information and strategic alignment, and the importance of having an effective assurance strategy, to help enable and optimize the achievement of the programme goals.

2.5.3 Transformational flow

Transformational flow is the term used to describe the lifecycle of the programme; it uses 'flow' to reflect the evolving nature of the journey the programme takes and the adjustments that will need to be made. The following list summarizes the stages it passes through (see Figure 2.4):

- **Identifying a Programme** takes an outline idea, and undertakes analysis of stakeholders, clarification of the strategic requirements and market consultation to turn it into a business concept that gains strategic support.
- **Defining a Programme** confirms the vision, undertakes detailed analysis of options and designs the programme infrastructure to deliver, resulting in a business case and strategic commitment.
- **Managing the Tranches** describes the cyclical activities involved in managing and proving the coordinating interface between projects, business change and strategic direction.
- **Delivering the Capability** explains how the alignment of the projects and other activities that deliver the blueprint will be managed and controlled.
- **Realizing the Benefits** outlines the preparing, delivering and reviewing activities that will take the capability delivered by projects, transition it into the business operations and embed it within the business operations to release the intended benefits.

■ **Closing a Programme** structures the end to the programme, consolidating and embedding the change, closing down all programme activity and completing stakeholder engagement.

2.5.4 Benefits of using MSP

If you are still not convinced, here are the main benefits of using MSP as the framework. MSP differentiates itself from other programme management frameworks because it really focuses on strategic change rather than more effective project delivery, coming at it from the top down rather than the bottom up.

The new version of MSP released in 2011 is double the size of the 2003 version, and the vast majority

of this increase is dedicated to the area of delivering business change and the role of the business change manager.

So, why should you consider using MSP as your programme management framework?

■ **It is flexible and adaptable** MSP is not a methodology that you implement; it needs to be adapted and applied carefully and thoughtfully. It may be that not all the elements of MSP will be needed in your organization and it can be blended to fit with other frameworks. If you are using PMI, APM (Association for Project Management) or PRINCE2® (PRojects IN Controlled Environments) for your project

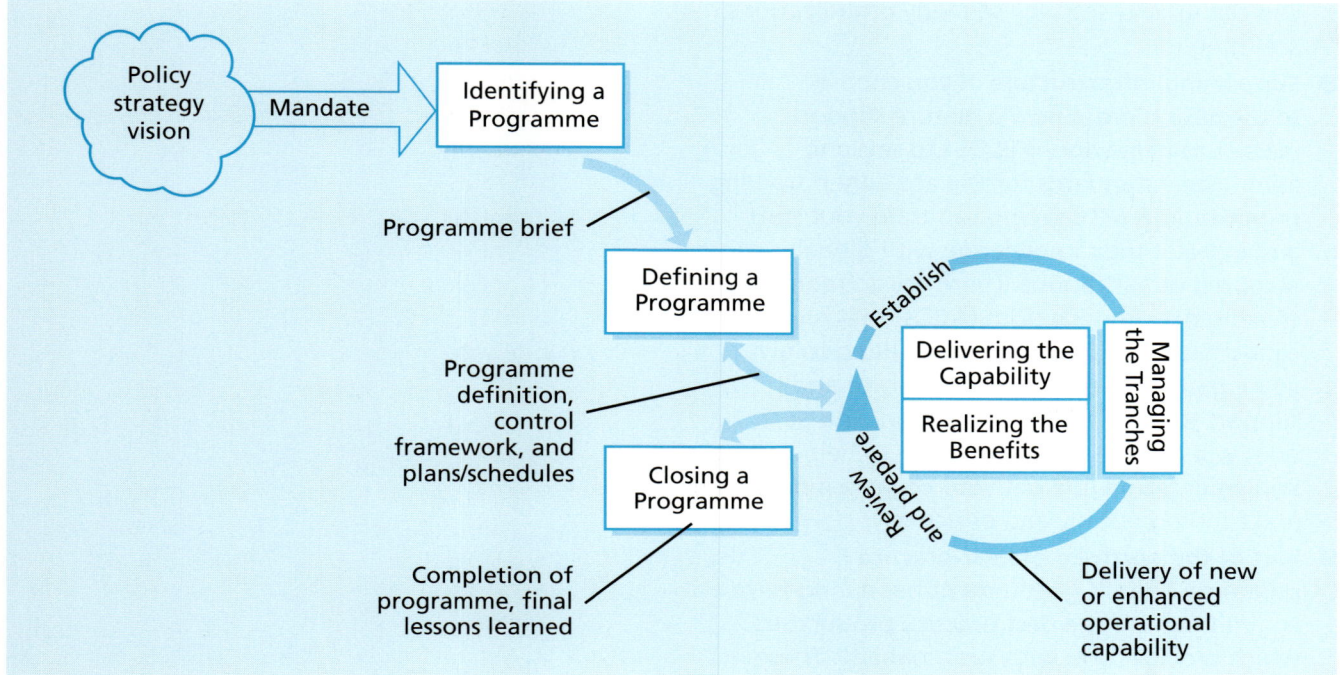

Figure 2.4 MSP transformational flow

management delivery, each will happily work with MSP.

- **It is proven and established** MSP has been around for more than 12 years now; it has been proven globally in the public and private sectors. Many of the problems identified from failed programmes would have been avoided if MSP had been applied. MSP is in a cycle of continual improvement and draws on knowledge and experiences as it evolves in one of the most rapidly changing industries.

- **Free to use without licensing constraints** Although AXELOS Ltd owns the intellectual property, there are very few constraints on its use or adoption. Compare this to the expensive programme management methods offered by the big consultancies and you can quickly see why so many organizations are using it.

- **Supporting infrastructure** If you choose to use MSP there is now a mature support market to help you. AXELOS Ltd sets and administers standards for the accredited training organizations (ATOs) who can train your staff and accredit their knowledge with globally accepted qualifications. There are accredited consultancy organizations (ACOs) that have consultants who have been accredited to give you impartial and high-quality advice and support to enable implementation. The best ones will be able to offer toolkits to help with implementation and get your organization up and running quickly and effectively.

- **Part of the portfolio of best-practice guidance** The UK government has a long-term commitment to the best-practice product set which provides you with sustainability. These products are becoming more and more consistent and are part of a cycle of improvements that will bring them more closely together.

There is an old saying 'No one ever got sacked for choosing IBM', and the same probably applies to the best-practice products. There is a well-established global industry that is enabling organizations using it to go from strength to strength. Hopefully, the five reasons listed above will provide you with the justification to set your strategic direction.

PART 2
Governance themes

Introduction to the governance themes

3

3 Introduction to the governance themes

'Organizations need to practise qualitative corporate governance rather than quantitative governance thereby ensuring it is properly run.'
Mervyn King

'You cannot legislate good behaviour.'
Mervyn King

The MSP governance themes are a set of references that explain how key elements of the programme should be delivered during its delivery lifecycle. They cover subjects that will need to be constantly managed, to a greater or lesser extent, on a daily basis during the lifecycle of the programme.

The nine MSP governance themes are dealt with in Chapters 4 to 11, but note that the order in which they are covered in this publication relates to the priorities of the business change manager rather than the order of the MSP guide. Visions and blueprints are combined in one chapter (Chapter 5).

The themes generally have a cycle of activities (see Figure 3.1). These are consistent and help us to understand some of the documentation, for example risk management. Risks will be identified and analysed, with the information recorded in the risk register. The plan to mitigate and manage the risks is then developed, the activities are undertaken and their effectiveness reviewed.

In the governance themes there will normally be one or more 'strategy' documents developed. These describe the cycle that will be followed, the responsibilities associated with that cycle, any processes and procedures that should be followed and any other relevant information on how the

programme wants the theme to be controlled and managed. The strategy document defines the framework that will operate for that theme, for example a risk management strategy.

From your perspective as a business change manager (BCM) you need to be very focused on these strategies (see Table 3.1), and ensure that they are developed and meet your needs. The MSP framework points the finger at the programme manager to create most of them, but you are a critical stakeholder and must be at the core of developing and understanding these strategies. You must not let them 'be done to you' by the programme team and you need to be taking a lead as the approach that is taken will be critical to enabling your success.

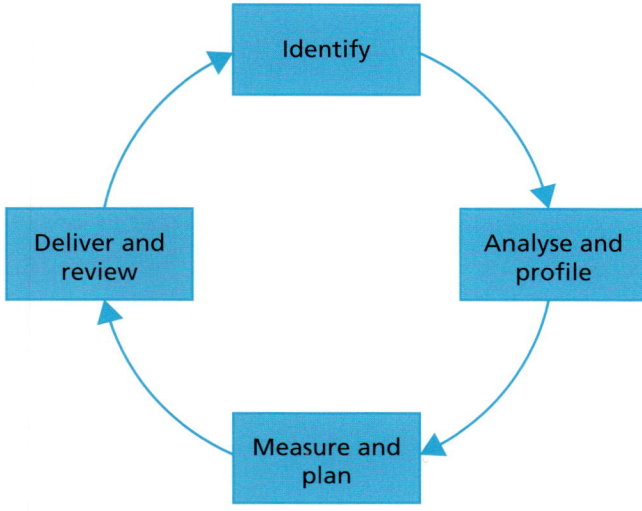

Figure 3.1 Typical theme lifecycle

Table 3.1 BCM engagement with strategy documents

Stakeholders engagement strategy	This defines how the stakeholders will be engaged and communications managed. It is critical to you as the outward-looking face of the programme and is a principal interface to stakeholders for the programme.
Resource management strategy	This outlines where the people to resource the programme are coming from. You are going to need the support of a change team, so you need to work out if they are going to be external or internal and how they are going to be released from the business.
Risk management strategy	You will need to ensure that operational risks are fully covered by the strategy. There is a danger that they will sit in a parallel environment, with the programme being focused on project-related matters: make sure that doesn't happen.
Issues management strategy	Generally this will tend to relate to programme and project delivery matters; however, issues to do with changing the organization, including staff resistance, will also follow the approach, so it needs to be flexible to your needs.
Quality and assurance strategy	This strategy may well be in line with your organization's assurance approach, but an area that you should keep an eye out for is assurance that your organization is actually prepared for the change. You need to have some mechanism in place for testing readiness.
Monitoring and control strategy	This strategy tends to be focused at the internal processes of the programme and how it controls its projects. Your main concern is that the projects will deliver their outputs on time and to the right standard, so you should think like a customer for this one.
Organization structure	This will include your terms of reference and those of your team so you need to be very active with this one. The structure of the programme will evolve through the various tranches and this document outlines how the structure will cope, as opposed to the resource management strategy, which outlines where the resources will come from.
Benefits management strategy	Although written by the programme manager, this document is at the core of your role in the programme. The programme manager should develop it because governance is their responsibility, but the actual content is yours. The strategy outlines how the benefits, which are your responsibility, will be achieved and measured.
Information management strategy	This strategy is concerned with the effectiveness of information management and the maintenance of its accuracy. From your perspective, this is important because you will need accurate data on business operational performance and benefits delivery. You should only commit to performance metrics where you are comfortable that the information can be made available.

In each of the themes there are a number of information sets being created, normally in the form of documents. They tend to involve a strategy, a profile or register relating to the specific content, and then a plan to deliver. The benefits theme (see Figure 3.2) provides a good example of how the documentation tends to work, although we have not covered the content of these documents in detail as this is dealt with in the MSP manual.

The benefits management strategy sets out the framework within which the programme will operate and deliver benefits.

The benefit profiles are the detailed descriptions of how each benefit will be achieved and measured. You do not want too many of these as it is better to have a small number of well-defined benefits than many diverse and not understood benefits.

The benefits realization plan is the tracking device to ensure your benefits appear and that they are proven and signed off.

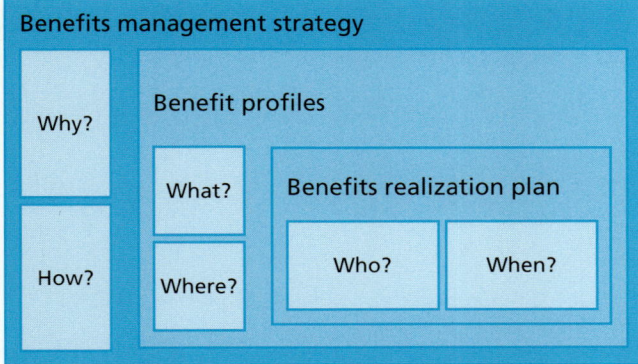

Figure 3.2 Benefits theme documentation

Programme organization 4

4   Programme organization

This chapter summarizes the MSP guidance on programme organization structures. It interprets the structure to help you work out how your responsibilities will be delivered, as the business change manager (BCM) role requires the most thoughtful interpretation.

4.1   BASIC PRINCIPLES

The programme governance model is relatively straightforward; it is a three-layer model of control (see Figure 4.1).

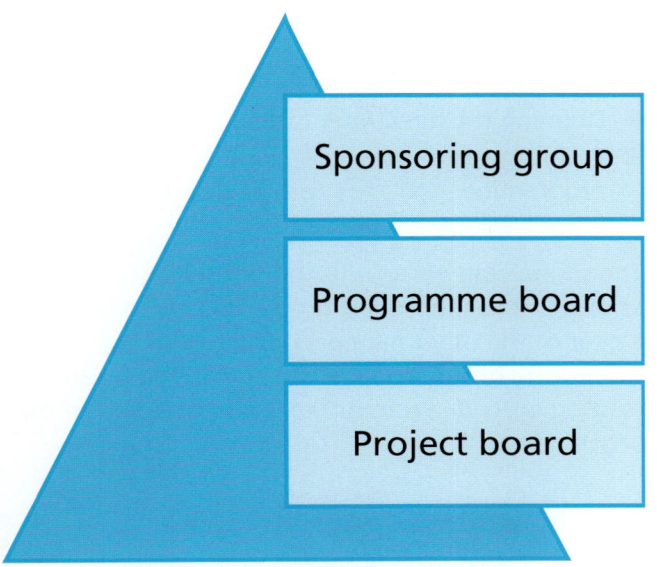

Figure 4.1 *Programme governance layers*

There is a sponsoring group that sits at the top of the structure and sets the strategic direction for the programme; increasingly these are being referred to as portfolio boards rather than sponsoring groups. They may have oversight over a number of programmes and endeavour to keep them aligned and optimized. It is highly likely that you will have a reporting line to a member of the sponsoring group.

The second tier is the group that is responsible for delivering the strategy or objective. This is called the programme board and it is where you sit in the organization. The programme board is responsible for delivering the new capability (normally through projects and transformation change activities) and, equally important, the anticipated benefits from the investment.

The third tier is the project, which normally has a control group, maybe referred to as the project board. There will be a number of these and this is where direct control of the projects is applied; this takes the strain off the programme board, which should be the escalation point when the projects have problems.

The relationship between core roles in MSP and these three layers of control is shown in Figure 4.2.

The senior responsible owner (SRO) is the interface to the sponsoring level, which could be the corporate or portfolio board; the names will vary between organizations. The SRO is accountable for achieving the strategy.

At the programme level, there is the programme manager, who should have direct control of the project resources and the programme team. Their role is principally to deliver the capability and manage the governance and controls of the programme.

The BCM, namely you, represents the areas to be changed, defining the requirements, designing how the organization will work in the future and delivering the dividend from the change, namely the benefits. In simple terms, you are the customer for what the programme will create, so you are critical in defining what will be required.

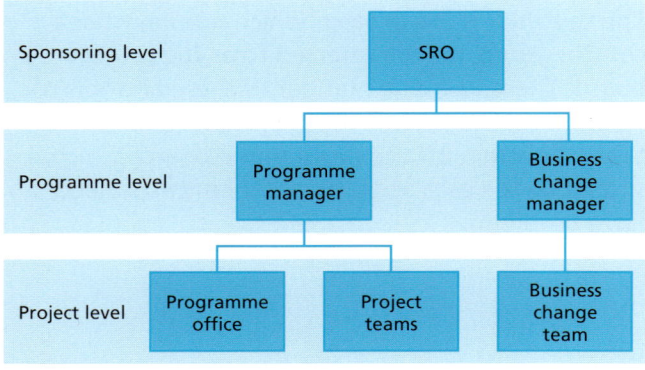

Figure 4.2 Programme roles

4.2 WHAT DOES MSP HAVE TO SAY?

Just for the record, we note below how MSP describes each of these roles. There is a long list of responsibilities for each of them in Chapter 4 of the full guide, but this summary captures the spirit of what it has to say.

4.2.1 Sponsoring group

The sponsoring group represents those senior managers who are responsible for:

- The investment decision
- Defining the direction of the business
- Ensuring the ongoing overall alignment of the programme with the strategic direction of the organization.

The sponsoring group will appoint the SRO who, as part of the sponsoring group, is likely to be a peer of the other members. The role of the sponsoring group may well be performed by an existing executive committee, or other board of the organization.

4.2.2 Senior responsible owner

The SRO is accountable for the programme, ensuring that it meets its objectives and realizes the expected benefits. The individual who fulfils this role should be able to lead the programme board with energy and drive, and must be empowered to direct the programme and take decisions. They must have enough seniority and authority to provide leadership to the programme team and take on accountability for delivery.

The BCM and programme manager are normally peers who report to the SRO (see Figure 4.3).

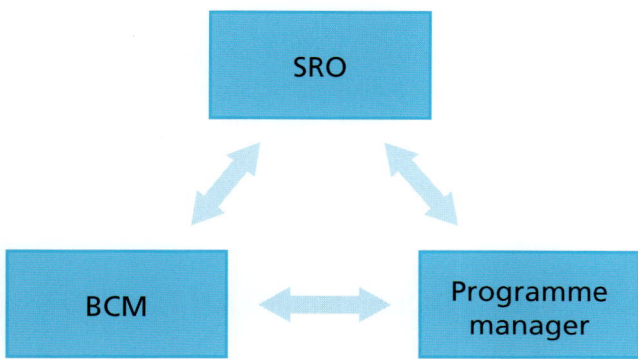

Figure 4.3 BCM and programme roles

4.2.3   Programme board

Established by the SRO (and often coming into existence following approval of the programme mandate, or possibly the programme brief), the prime purpose of the programme board will be to drive the programme forward and deliver the outcomes and benefits. Members will provide resources and specific commitment to support the SRO, who is accountable for the successful delivery of the programme.

The programme board reports to the SRO. While the SRO may delegate responsibilities and action to members of the programme board; its existence does not dilute the SRO's accountabilities and decision-making authority.

Programme board members must take the lead in supporting the authority and control of the SRO

over the programme as a whole, including ensuring appropriate coordination across the projects and activities that comprise the programme.

4.2.4   Programme manager

The programme manager is responsible for leading and managing the programme from establishing the programme through to delivery of the new capabilities, realization of benefits and programme closure. The programme manager has primary responsibility for successful delivery of the new capabilities and establishing governance. The BCM is responsible for benefits realization via the organizational adoption and usage of the capability and transition to the desired outcome.

The programme manager will normally be appointed as part of forming the team for Defining a Programme, though it is important that someone assumes the role of programme manager when the programme brief and plans for programme definition (programme preparation plan) are being developed in Identifying a Programme.

4.2.5   Business change manager

The role of the BCM is primarily benefits- and change-focused. The BCM is responsible, on behalf of the business operations and the SRO, for:

■ Defining the benefits
■ Defining the future operating state of the business area they represent
■ Assessing progress towards Realizing the Benefits
■ Achieving measured improvements
■ Monitoring performance.

The programme needs to define and realize benefits in terms of measured improvements in business performance, which means that the BCM must be 'business-side' in order to provide a bridge between the programme and business operations.

The programme manager is responsible for Delivering the Capability, while the BCM is responsible for Realizing the [resultant] Benefits by embedding that capability into business operations and facilitating business changes to exploit that capability. The individuals appointed to each role must be able to work in close partnership to ensure that the right capabilities are delivered and that they are put to best use.

If a programme is implementing change across different parts of an organization, market or socio-economic environment, a BCM should represent the diverse nature of the impact. An integral part of the BCM's role is an intimate knowledge of, and credibility in, the groups that are to be changed.

4.2.6   Business change team

A business change team can be formed to help each of the BCMs take their stakeholders in their operational areas through the change cycle. Such a team considers the interests of those parts of the organization to be changed and will ensure that they are thoroughly prepared for the transition. The team's focus is on helping the operational unit through transition as smoothly as possible. It is a support function for when operational people need the most help.

4.2.7   Programme office

Programmes are major undertakings, often affecting large numbers of people and organizations and generating a substantial volume of information. The nerve centre and information hub of a programme is the programme office. All information, communication, monitoring and control activities for the programme are coordinated through the programme office.

4.2.8   Programme assurance

Assurance is the assessment of specific aspects to generate confidence that the programme is being managed effectively and that it is on track to realize the expected benefits and achieve the desired outcomes. Assurance, like audit, should be carried out independently of the programme management team; this may be by either an internal team and/or an external review team. A key role of assurance is to identify potential problems before they arise.

4.3   WHAT DOES THIS MEAN TO YOU?

Hopefully, the sections above have given a sense of where your role sits in the programme's structure and that it is pivotal in achieving programme success. When programmes start up often the energy and dialogue are concerned with launching projects and the whole business change issue is generally ignored as it is months or years away. The flaw in this logic is that it means change isn't thought about until it is too late, at which point failure looms.

4.3.1   Your title

The term BCM has been in MSP for many years but is not appropriate for all situations. The MSP authors have struggled to find an alternative so have stuck with this one.

Some scenarios where the title of BCM may not seem appropriate include the following:

■ Your pay grade may be above manager (e.g. you are a director).

■ It may not be a business that is being changed; it could be a social economic programme and it is societal change.

■ You may have responsibility for delivering some sort of external market restructuring.

■ You may be representing a significant supply chain partner (e.g. the outsourced ICT supplier).

There are numerous other scenarios where you may be required to sit on a programme board with the BCM hat on, and find the title doesn't quite seem to fit. The answer to this is relatively simple; change the title to fit what is most appropriate, but don't lose the core principle that the BCM delivers transformational change.

Alternative words to 'business' could be 'structure', 'market', 'social', 'environment' or 'partnership'. Try to leave the word 'change' in place though you could use 'transformation', and alternatives to 'manager' could be 'director', 'authority', 'leader', 'champion' or 'executive'.

> **Hints and tips**
>
> Try to avoid the word 'owner' in relation to MSP as it is pretty meaningless and has been largely removed from the main guide for exactly that reason.

4.3.2 Your new role

Once you have the title, the next challenge is to find out what the role really does and what competencies you will need to have.

Hopefully, the chief who has invited you to take this role of BCM will have been a member of the sponsoring group or corporate management team. The chief will also have discussed the BCM role with the SRO, as you will have a reporting line to them.

It could be the SRO who has approached you; this is quite common. Whatever the scenario, you need to be clear about why you have been nominated and who you report to.

It will be helpful if you have a sense of humour to go with your ambition, because the BCM role is one of the toughest to find the right people for. The programme and project teams can be recruited from the external market but it is not so easy to buy in BCMs who have intricate knowledge of an organization or sector. They have to come from within the organization as they need to know how it functions, the politics, the culture and the amount of change that can be driven through without causing performance to deteriorate.

You will be expected to perform as an effective transformational leader of change, and to achieve this you will need to:

■ Have the respect of the parts of the organization or sector you represent

■ Establish effective working relationships with other senior managers on the programme board

■ Have personal belief in the strategy and objectives; if not, you will become a saboteur

■ Be able to sell the concepts to a wide range of stakeholders and set appropriate expectations

■ Have the self-belief to challenge direction if you do not believe the benefits and outcomes are achievable; it's better to stop now than fail later

■ Be politically astute.

To be an effective manager of change you will also need to be able to:

■ Control adequate resources to achieve your responsibilities

■ Manage time and performance effectively to cope with the pressure for change

- Communicate effectively with programme and project staff
- Negotiate effectively with your peers to achieve preferred solutions
- Build, manage and motivate a team
- Understand and manage the implications for operational performance
- Have the time available, or a replacement who will do your day job.

4.3.3 Your day job

This is a particular challenge as your credibility for the role is almost certainly linked to your position in the organization, which probably gives you the authority to make many of the changes.

The role in the programme will impose significant demands on your time, which may already be stretched by the demands of your day job. As a minimum you should expect to spend between 20 and 60% of your time dedicated to programme management work. In reality it may be more than that and could be anything up to full time, so it is likely you will need backup to cover your day job.

A key element of being a successful BCM is ensuring that you remain in contact with what is happening on the ground. You must be careful not to become too detached. You may have people who are full time on the programme doing the work, but as the BCM you should try to maintain the interest of your main role as a key senior manager.

The reality is that you will almost certainly require a team to support you in both roles. There may be opportunities to provide people with more day-to-day responsibilities to release you for the programme role and you may bring in some dedicated change management expertise to work more fully with the programme.

It is important that the BCM is not fully dedicated to the programme as this will diminish your authority and influence in the organization. The BCM is a gatekeeper between the programme and the organization areas to be changed, so you must have ongoing credibility and trust on both sides. You are also going to need to balance the rate of change driven by the programme with the stability required to maintain business performance targets (see Figure 4.4).

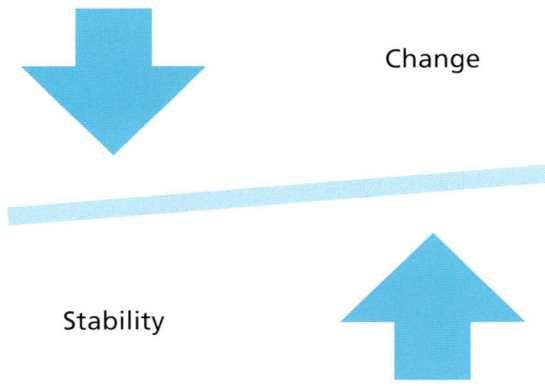

Figure 4.4 Keeping the balance

4.4 YOUR RELATIONSHIP WITH THE OTHER ROLES IN A PROGRAMME

The relationships in a programme are complex (see Figure 4.5). The list below provides a quick summary of your relationship with the main roles and groups:

- **Sponsoring group** You are likely to have a reporting line into one of the executives who is sponsoring the programme and you will be looking after their interests in the programme. You will probably have a direct report to someone on this group.
- **Senior responsible owner** The SRO is accountable to the sponsoring group for the successful achievement of the programme objectives; your

job is to support them in that role and ensure that the change management controls are in place to keep them out of trouble.

■ **Programme manager** The programme manager is a fellow member of the programme board and has day-to-day responsibility for the effective running of the programme. They are the mirror image of your role as they deliver the capability to you and you take that capability and deliver the benefits. In many respects you are the customer of the programme manager, as you define what is needed to achieve the benefits and then they build it for you.

■ **Other BCMs** The potential for conflict here should not be underestimated. The needs of different parts of the organization or market are often in conflict and the BCMs will need to resolve these conflicts to their own satisfaction to ensure that it is clear what is required from each

programme. Without this, programme boards will become places of significant conflict if there are competing demands that cannot be resolved.

■ **Programme office** The programme office supports the programme manager in managing the projects in the same way as the business change team supports you. However, you will need to build a good relationship with them because they are the knowledge hub of the programme and will know where the issues are that may affect you. They will need information from you about stakeholders, risks, issues and business performance data; they will also be a good source of information for you on the progress of projects and potential issues that may arise.

■ **Programme assurance** The people doing programme assurance are your friends and it is much better to keep on good terms with them so

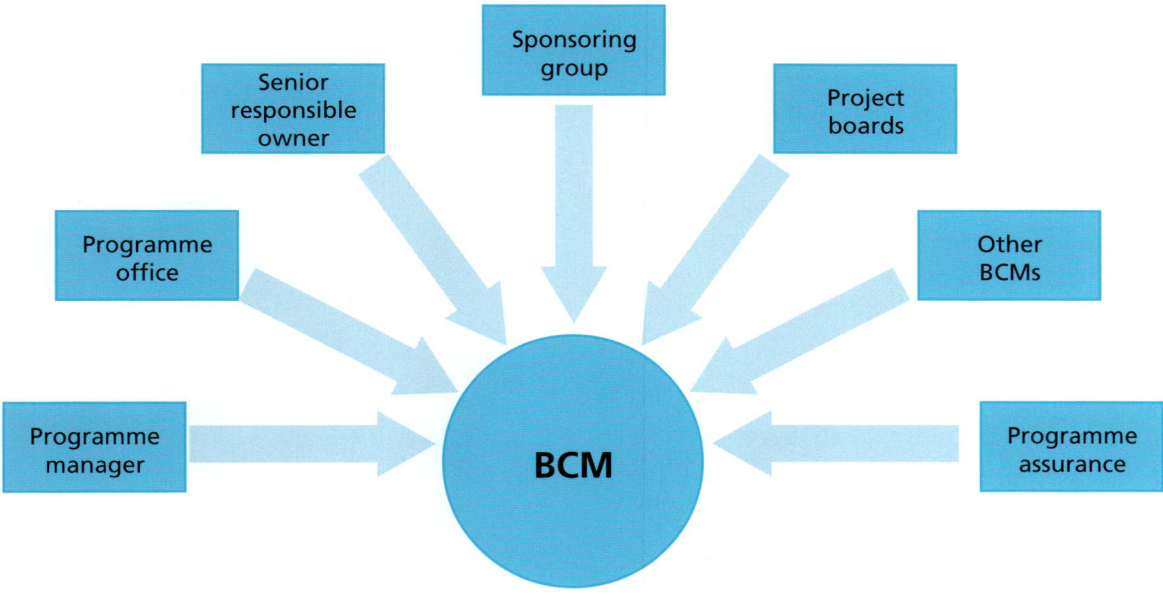

Figure 4.5 The BCM and other roles

they can help you. They will give you advice and guidance on the best approaches to handling problems and you can use them to undertake reviews of the readiness to change and make sure you are not being misled about how advanced preparations are.

■ **Project boards** Your relationship with project boards can be complex and vary a lot. You may end up being a project executive for some projects that affect you and where you want to be directly in control. In other circumstances a senior user role may be more appropriate. Boards offer a great opportunity to include other managers in shaping the change by nominating them to represent you as senior users. You may also have a role in supplying resources to support the delivery of the projects; this may be achieved by nominating members of your business change team to represent you.

4.5   ESTABLISHING THE BUSINESS CHANGE TEAM

When forming your business change team there are a number of factors you should take into account in designing the structure, your role and the team around you. As you are reading this guide it is likely that there will not be a lot of experience within the organization to draw on or use as a template, so hopefully the following will help.

4.5.1   Your terms of reference

You must have terms of reference that are meaningful, relevant to the role and agreed with the SRO. The MSP guide has a never-ending list of generic responsibilities, but you need something much more specific. The following checklist provides questions that your terms of reference should answer:

■ What resources are being put under your control: human, financial and physical?
■ How much time are you expected to dedicate to the role each week and for how long?
■ Who do you report to and will the relationship work?
■ What level of specific responsibilities will you have for:
  ● Stop/go decisions on change and transition
  ● Communications and stakeholder activities
  ● Benefits (both within areas you have specific responsibility for and in areas that are not specifically under your control)
  ● Operational risk management
  ● Staff and industrial relations
  ● Sustaining corporate performance metrics
  ● Assembling and authorizing the blueprint
  ● Business case achievement.

4.5.2   The structure

There are many potential models that you can deploy; however, there are some core functions

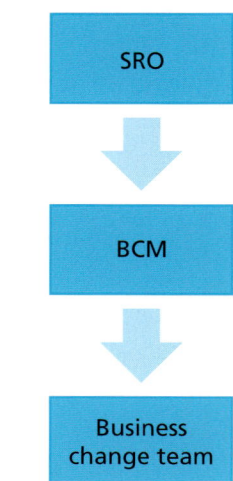

Figure 4.6 Direct line of sight

that the business change team must perform and therefore in some shape or form you should have resources in place to cover these.

There is direct line of sight (see Figure 4.6) from the SRO, who is accountable for the programme, to you and your team, as your role and this team are fundamental to achieving the successful changes required by the programme objectives.

The checklist below provides questions that will help you define what you require in your business team and how much:

- How well documented is the current operating status? Will it need to be documented or does that documentation already exist?
- Will communications be the responsibility of this team or some other group?
- Have you got the subject matter expertise (e.g. contract management as opposed to procurement (which the programme will manage) or specifications expertise) to ensure that what is provided will meet your requirements?
- How will information be distributed? Is there an existing infrastructure or will one have to be designed?
- Is there currently monitoring of performance or will a process and information need to be developed?
- What will the projects and programme be expecting from the team?
- Will any tools and systems be required to help the team?
- What internal resources will be available?
- What experience of this kind of change does the organization have?
- What level of external change expertise and advice will be required?

- How will the team expand and contract during the programme lifecycle?

4.5.3 Building the capability

Once you have worked through your own role and the team structure then you will need to think about building the capability of the team. The nature of the programme and previous experience of this sort will largely dictate how much investment will be required to build the capability; below are some areas you should consider.

Skills and training will almost certainly be required and are often ignored. The team will need to have a good understanding of change management, at the organizational, team and individual levels. There are many approaches that can provide excellent foundation knowledge upon which to build, so various concepts that you should consider and the reasons for including them are grouped and listed below.

Individual change management concepts:

- Elizabeth Kübler-Ross bereavement curve, because it shows that adapting to change takes time and is emotional
- Kirton's Adaption–Innovation (KAI), because it shows that people have quite distinct information needs and responses to change, which has an impact on how communications need to be created (to meet both types)
- McGregor's Theory X and Theory Y management styles, because they are practical and include a lot of other theories (Maslow, Humanistic, Behavioural).

Team change management theories:

- Glaser and Glaser's five elements of team effectiveness, because it is practical and applies to all teams regardless of performance.

Organization change management theories:

- Lewin's three-stage models (unfreeze, move, freeze), because it is very similar to the two-stage model in the Realizing the Benefits process
- Kotter's eight-step model, because it is widely accepted and proven
- Senge's model, because it is an agile approach
- Senge's three types of leader, because one of the types is the BCM and it will help you to see what leadership you should expect from other roles (line managers and sponsors)
- Goleman's emotional competencies, because it is a very useful toolkit for a BCM.

Technical skills to support the programme include:

- Process mapping and documentation
- Benefits management
- Planning
- Business performance management, and modelling techniques such as Lean and Six Sigma
- Stakeholder and communications management
- Project controls
- Risk management
- Technical knowledge of the change, the market or particular products or technology.

There are specific BCM courses available that would normally cover most of these concepts in an integrated fashion. The Centre for Change Management offers a BCM Practitioner qualification (see www.c4cm.co.uk).

Team building and development is often overlooked when assembling temporary teams. A programme may well be in place for some years and will need to establish values of its own. It will also be subject to regular change as different people are moved into and out from the team during the programme lifecycle, so the team must be adaptable to change itself.

Using team change management concepts provides a good opportunity to work out how to get the best out of the team. Why not consider doing a Myers–Briggs or The Colour Works personality assessment of the individuals to see how they fit together and the likely effect on interactions? Ideally this should be done as part of the recruitment process so issues are identified early. Many organizations have their own preferred techniques and methods for this kind of analysis so you should use whatever your own organization prefers.

4.6 YOUR CHECKLIST FOR SETTING UP THE PROGRAMME ORGANIZATION

This is what MSP describes as the 'areas of focus' in relation to the programme organization (see Table 4.1). In practice this means things you and the others listed below should do.

With **other BCMs** you should consider what resources can be shared and those that are specific to your area.

With the **programme manager** you should consider what skills will be in the programme office and within the project teams that you will need to call on.

With the **SRO** you should work to gain the approval for your structure and resourcing plan.

Table 4.1 Programme organization areas of focus

Role	Area of focus
Senior responsible owner (SRO)	Ensuring that the programme has the necessary skills, resources and experience required to deliver the change
	Putting clear lines of authority in place
	Ensuring that sponsoring group members have a clear understanding of their roles
	Appointment of the programme manager
	Approval of the BCM appointment by the sponsoring group members
Programme manager	Design and appointment of the programme team
	Appointment of the programme office
	Facilitating the appointment of project management teams
	Ensuring that all roles have clearly defined responsibilities
	Ensuring that the organization design is managed through the programme lifecycle
	Induction of new members into the programme team
	Line management of the programme team
	Efficiency and competency of resources being deployed
Business change manager(s)	Design and appointment of the business change team
	Induction and management of members into the business change team
	Development and performance of the individuals in the business change team
Programme office	Advice and guidance on roles and responsibilities within the programme team
	Maintenance of organization information
	Support in recruitment and appointments

Visions and
blueprints

5

5 Visions and blueprints

'If we don't know where we are going, how will we know when we have arrived let alone how we are going to get there?' Yendor Nedwos

Visions and blueprints are very important concepts as they set out the strategic direction for the programme and help to mobilize the change and provide the clarity about what the programme will actually deliver.

The vision has two aspects: there is the 'vision' that sets out the justification for the programme and what the world will be like at the end, and there is also the 'vision statement', which encapsulates the vision into a statement that provides the basis of communications. The vision may be expressed in different ways, so there may actually be different versions of the vision statement to meet the needs of different audiences. It is important that there is only one vision as there can only be one ending.

The blueprint is the definition of what the programme will deliver; it can also be referred to as the target operating model, but care needs to be taken with this term. There are many interpretations of the term 'target operating model' and there are many examples which definitely do not match up to the expectations of a programme blueprint.

The term 'outcomes' is used liberally in business speech. As a point of clarity, in programme management the outcomes are what happens when the blueprint comes to life. So, if the programme is talking about the outcomes it will deliver, then the blueprint should contain the detail behind these

outcomes; if the blueprint doesn't exist at this stage, you may already be in trouble.

MSP deals with these concepts separately but in this publication they are covered together as they are inherently linked. There is also a link to benefits (see Figure 5.1) but benefits management is covered separately in Chapter 6. These three concepts are at the core of the business change manager (BCM) role.

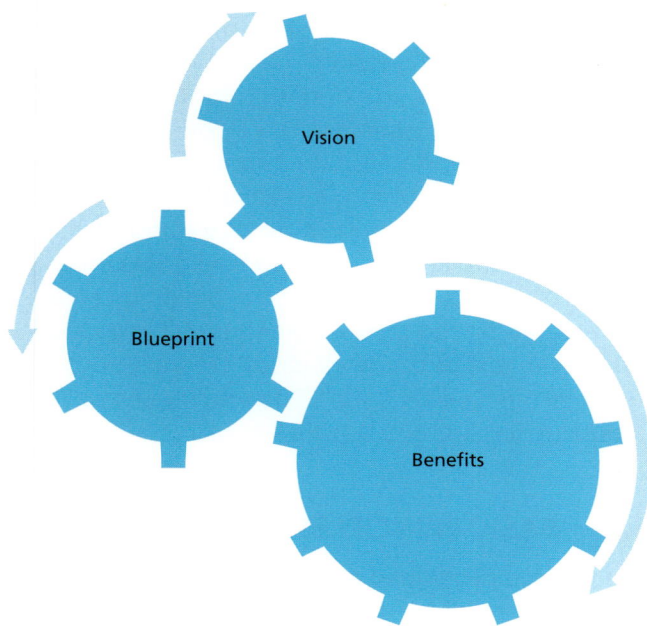

Figure 5.1 Vision, blueprint and benefits

Example

Imagine you are on one of the TV property makeover shows. You have just bought a run-down building and believe you can turn it into your dream home (your vision). You are not an architect or a builder, so you will need the help of these professionals. You will need to describe your dream home to the architect. What do you expect back – artist impressions or similar? When these are correct you have a vision statement. These can be used to help the builder and your family understand what the end result will look like.

The architect will need to develop designs for the builders. The starting point has to be understanding the current state of the building. This is the 'as-is' blueprint. The artist's impressions need to become a proper design for the building when it will be completed. This is the 'to-be' or final-state blueprint. But wait, you need to move into the property before it is complete and to sell your existing house to raise funds to finish the job. So the architect is going to have to produce a design showing how some of the building can be completed first to give you adequate living space while the rest of the work is carried out. This is an intermediate blueprint. The two phases of construction are two tranches in MSP.

5.1 BASIC PRINCIPLES

The vision is developed early in the programme and this is one of the main reasons that the BCM needs to be in place at the outset. If the vision is established without your involvement, then it may be difficult for you to buy into it. If you aren't committed to the vision, you are not going to make a very effective BCM.

A good way to describe the role of the vision is that it acts as a 'beacon' for the programme, setting out the direction and justification for the change.

Example

There was a programme in the UK fire service to implement regional emergency call centres. The BCMs on the programme board were exactly the right people, with the right authority to undertake the role. However, the programme was politically driven and had no blueprint that defined how it would work or benefits to justify the change. The BCMs were unconvinced at the start and, as the programme began to lose momentum, they became more convinced it wouldn't work and lost any belief in the vision. The programme failed at significant loss to the taxpayer.

The blueprint is the flip side of the vision; whereas the vision is setting out where the programme is going, the blueprint describes what it will be like when the programme arrives. It is where the detail of what will be left behind by the programme is stored.

The blueprint is your key document as it defines the difference between where you are today and the end state, which is the change you have to deliver. It details what services will be provided, how and who will provide them, what infrastructure needs to be in place and the information that will be used to manage it.

A common cause for programme failure is the lack of a blueprint, which means that the programme doesn't really know where it is going. The programme launches projects hopefully but there comes a point of revelation when someone realizes it doesn't all add up – quite often that someone is a

BCM and by then too much money has been spent badly.

So, the blueprint is critical; it is the document that contains the definition of what your functions will look like after the change and it is essential that you own the detail. Without a blueprint it is not possible to effectively estimate benefits or what capability you will need delivered by the projects. Summary information about the projects that will be required is stored in a document called the projects dossier.

For specification-led programmes there is a temptation to focus totally on the structure: digging the tunnel or building the technology. This isn't surprising as this is where the money will be spent. However, the focus needs to be on how the programme will be managed and where the benefits will come from.

Business transformation programmes often focus on process and supply chain redesign, so there is clarity about the end game. There may be some ambiguity and the options need to be identified and tracked.

Socio-economic programmes need to define the behaviour and structural changes that will be required as well as the infrastructure that will need to be put into place to support the new *modus operandi*.

The blueprint contains key sets of information upon which the programme design and delivery will be based:

- The 'as-is' state – how the parts of the organization that will be changed work at present.
- The 'to-be' state – how the organization will work when the programme has completed.
- Intermediate states – how the organization will be working at major control points (tranches in the MSP guide) during the lifecycle of the programme.

The blueprint itself can be constructed in a number of ways, using organization charts, flowcharts, process diagrams, soft systems mapping, and technical diagrams covering buildings, IT, information flows and so on.

A programme is a long journey. When planning any journey there are some critical factors to consider:

- Where are you starting from? The 'as-is' blueprint.
- Where is your journey's end, and how will you know when you have arrived? The 'to-be' final blueprint.
- It's a long journey, so where do you need to stop en route and for what – fuel, toilets, drink, food?

These stops en route are like the intermediate blueprints. Could you complete a long journey without them? No, of course you couldn't, so don't expect a programme to be any different.

5.2   WHAT DOES MSP HAVE TO SAY?

The following sections are brief extracts from MSP that outline what the main guide says on the topic.

5.2.1   Vision

A vision is a picture of a better future; it is the basis for the outcomes and delivered benefits of the programme. As such it is a vital focus and enabler for the buy-in, motivation and activity alignment of the large community of people involved in any programme.

The vision statement is used to communicate the end goal of the programme, being a summary impression of the desired future state.

Characteristics of a good vision statement can be summarized as follows:

- It is written as a future state. It is not to be confused with an objective, strategy, intention or mission, all of which could begin with the word 'to'. Instead, it is a snapshot of the organization in the future.
- It can be easily understood by a wide variety of stakeholders; it is easy to communicate. This means it does not use jargon understood by only one group. It is clear in the vision statement how this better future is different from the present.
- It is written with the broadest groupings of stakeholders as the target audience.
- It describes a compelling future that engages the heart as well as the head. This does not mean it is emotional, but nor is it dry and factual.
- It sets out the current reality as part of the justification for the change – that is, why the organization cannot stay where it is.
- It matches the degree of transformation change with the boldness of the vision conveyed. Vision statements should motivate everyone and need to do justice to the challenge of transformational change.
- It avoids target dates unless the vision is truly time dependent.
- It describes a desirable future, in terms of the interests of key stakeholders. Key benefits are implicit.
- It describes a vision that is verifiable but without too many detailed performance targets. A vision statement that contains an inspirational future that is not verifiable can breed scepticism among stakeholders. It should be clear when the organization has arrived at the future state.

- It is sufficiently flexible to remain relevant over the life of the programme. It does not contain too many constraints.
- It provides sufficient context and direction to enable the development of the blueprint.

The statement needs to be short and memorable but relevant. Some of the best vision statements are no more than a few words long.

The vision underpins communications, and is communicated repeatedly at all kinds of events. Ideally, stakeholders should be able to recall it from memory almost word for word.

5.2.2 Blueprint

The programme's vision provides a description of the desired outcomes in customer-focused terms. As the vision is a description at a summary level it needs to be expanded and developed into a blueprint, which evolves and is refined during the lifecycle of the programme. It is the blueprint that provides a basis for modelling benefits and designing the projects dossier. Figure 5.2 shows how the MSP design documents fit together.

The blueprint is not concerned with how to get to the future state. The 'how' is dealt with when designing the projects dossier. A number of scenarios will be considered for the final outcome of the programme along with the options for delivering these scenarios. The optimum outcomes and options for delivering these outcomes are selected. This is reviewed over the programme lifecycle to ensure the outcomes and solutions remain optimal.

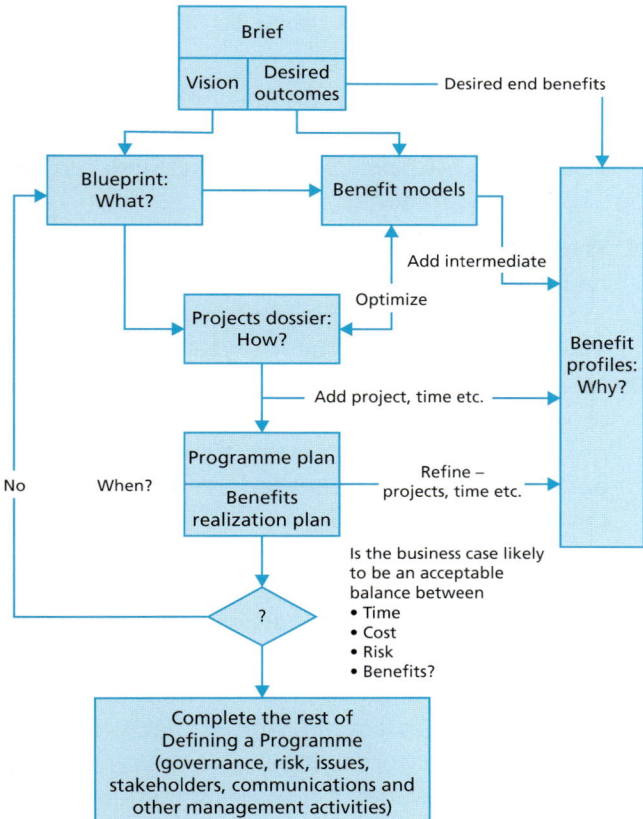

Figure 5.2 MSP design documents

The new capability occurs when the outputs from projects are put into operational use; once transition is completed the outcomes have been achieved and benefits can be realized.

The programme manager is responsible for organizing activities to ensure the blueprint is appropriately authored and owned. Where the programme manager and BCM have suitable skills and experience, they can be the authors of the blueprint. Where they don't, it is the responsibility of the programme manager, assisted by the BCM,

to engage appropriately skilled and knowledgeable people as the authors.

The POTI model sets a high-level scope of what must be included and integrated in an effective blueprint:

- **P** Processes, business models of operations and functions including operational costs and performance levels
- **O** Organizational structure, staffing levels, roles, skills requirements, organizational culture, supply chain and style
- **T** Technology, buildings, IT systems and tools, equipment, machinery and accommodation
- **I** Information and data required for the future business operations and performance measurement

Each programme has to plan and manage the journey from the current operating model to the future operating model as described in the vision statement. An understanding of the current state and the gap (the difference between current and future states) is essential to be able to effectively explore alternative approaches to delivering the new capability.

The initial analysis of the gap is a comparison between the current organization (described in the 'current state' section of the blueprint) and the design for the future organization (described in the 'future state' section of the blueprint).

Elements of the blueprint, such as processes, technology etc., are compared as they are now with how they need to be. More detailed analysis will be carried out by projects, but there should be enough detail in the blueprint to be able to provide the business requirements for the projects.

5.3 WHAT DOES THIS MEAN TO YOU?

'Without leaps of imagination, or dreaming, we lose the excitement of possibilities. Dreaming, after all, is a form of planning.' Gloria Steinem

The creation of a blueprint for the future operation of the organization or sector is at the heart of the BCM role. It is also one of the more difficult things to deliver as it challenges people to think through the consequences of the vision, which may not be particularly pleasant and will identify decisions that people would rather not have to make.

Because of this, it is often easier to put the task of creating a blueprint to one side and get on with something more 'urgent' and less challenging. The problem with that is the blueprint never gets done, which means there is no clarity about what the projects need to deliver or where and how the benefits will materialize.

There are a number of fundamental reasons why blueprints don't get written. These can be summarized as:

- Inexperience of the programme team and leadership, who do not understand the need for it
- Just-do-it approach to programme delivery – let's get busy and see where we end up
- Programmes being run by project people who have no experience or knowledge of business modelling or change
- Lack of clarity within the programme or the organization on where it is going and the process of blueprinting asks too many difficult questions
- Assumption that someone has already done it and knows where you are going.

5.3.1 What do you need to do about the vision

Programmes are often big on the vision. Visions may come in many shapes and forms and have varying degrees of success. Some of the weaker ones can be put into these categories:

- **The to-do list** A list of things that need to happen to achieve something. Such visions tend to focus on the obvious and often lack longevity and come to a stop in the first year.
- **Mission statement** Some blunt statements which sound good are not really a foundation for a programme. These statements tend to define what will happen, rather than the direction or destination.
- **Management waffle** A few sentences that are vague enough so that key stakeholders can agree, but have little relevance to what needs to happen or nobody is really sure what they mean.
- **Sermon** This kind of vision goes on for quite a long time, makes lots of promises that can't be achieved or measured, but excites some people for some of the time. It provides something for everyone but very little for most.
- **Rich pictures** These are quite often innovative and expensive. They can be very good at explaining the vision and the journey, though they can also sometimes be quite obscure and a bit cryptic (see Figure 5.3 for an example).

The majority of vision statements aren't really fit for the job. If anything they are a tick in a box to get the programme moving rather than focusing on the end game and very few provide the basis for a blueprint. So here are a few tips on how to pull together a decent vision statement that has longevity.

Figure 5.3 Example of a rich picture

Gather together the following information on which to build the vision statement:

- Drivers and justification for the programme
- Type of programme – compliance, vision-led or emergent?
- 'Must do' outcomes and any deadlines
- Services that will be changed, stopped or started
- Structural changes to the organization, market and supply chain
- Technology, infrastructure, legislation or property changes that are anticipated
- Values which need to be included that are close to the organization's heart (e.g. environmental sustainability)

Creating the statement will depend on the organization, but don't be scared to make a few strong statements that stand alone. That is often easier than crafting a page of words. A statement on each of the above setting a positive, ambitious

position would be a good start. To test that you have done a decent job, use the following checklist:

- Will it make sense to the stakeholders it is intended for?
- Does it clarify the current reality and justification for change?

Example

A great vision statement came from a director in the UK National Health Service (NHS). After listening to the principles of MSP and realizing that the first job was to sort out the vision, she said 'Well, we've got to do it, so we had better mop up all the other things that are going on and do the best for the community while we are at it.' In one line she has recognized that they have a compliance programme, which had an element of 'emergent' in it, and then she set out a vision beyond both compliance and emergent.

- Will it survive changes of scope and timescales?
- Can you develop a blueprint from it?
- Will it act as the beacon and underpin decision-making?

5.3.2 What do you need to do about the blueprint?

One of the problems is actually knowing where to start with the blueprint, as potentially it is a large document, highly complex and technical.

Don't make the mistake of thinking that POTI (process, organization, technology, information) are heading boxes into which to feed information. The blueprint is derived from what the organization does now and what it will do in the future, so there must be clarity about how the elements fit together.

The first thing to remember is that a blueprint will not be created overnight. It is most likely that one or two people will need to be dedicated to the task, and it will evolve as the programme understanding develops. Creating a blueprint may require specialist skills and knowledge (e.g. enterprise design and business analysis skills rather than programme and change management skills).

The second thing to remember is confidentiality. While there will be much enthusiasm about developing and communicating the vision, the reality and detail of what is being planned will be stored in the blueprint with potentially much sensitive detail about structures, markets and other information that you may not wish to be communicated.

Each BCM should create a blueprint for the areas they are responsible for. These need to be in a common format so that they can be overlaid

Example

A review of a programme brief for an Australian government department appeared to show that the programme team had done a good job of outlining a detailed set of outcomes for the programme. These had been presented to the sponsoring group who had rejected them, saying that they wanted something different.

What had actually happened was that the team had presented the future very clearly, but had focused on the difficult issues. The sponsoring group blamed the MSP approach rather than confronting the fact that they didn't want to deal with difficult issues.

and compared at a later date. If they are written differently they will be incompatible and a waste of time. The aim is for a single blueprint for the programme and there is a real need for pragmatism. The blueprint is likely to be constructed from a mix of formats ranging from flow diagrams to description documents.

Once the blueprint has been developed it will almost certainly evolve, but this must be controlled, as changes to the blueprint will affect the projects and the potential benefits.

5.3.3 How does it work now?

The POTI framework from MSP (see earlier in this chapter) is very useful, but it isn't always the best place to start as very few organizations really know what their processes are. Despite all the rhetoric most organizations depend on people's behaviour and what they need to get done rather than the process they are supposed to follow.

Table 5.1 Simple example POTI for a garage

Process	Technology	Organization	Information
Bookings	Telephone	Administrator	Tester availability
	Diary system		Test bay schedule
Testing	Ramp	MOT tester	Testing schedule
	Rolling road	Assistant	Test report
	Calibrators		Failure report
	Testing bay		Approved
Certification	VOSA system	MOT tester	Pass/fail rates
	Stamp	Supervisor	Certificate to customer

The starting point is to ask the question 'What is it that we do now and how is it done?', which is the 'as-is' state in the blueprint.

It is surprising what will come out of this, but it will be in a language that everyone understands rather than technical terms that turn people off. The right people need to be involved; they must be the ones that know how things work now, in reality not theoretically.

One of the key reasons for defining the 'as-is' state is to fully understand the extent of the change and ensure that no unforeseen gaps appear during transition.

Table 5.1 is a very simple example of a POTI for a garage that undertakes vehicle testing. The service has three processes (bookings, testing and certification), and at the basic level Table 5.1 shows all that is needed to do the 'as-is' state.

Even from a very simple POTI such as that shown in Table 5.1 you can see the effect of making a change on the existing services, particularly if elements are being taken away.

Example

A good example of the value of an 'as-is' approach was a global banking group in the UK that was re-tendering its building contracts. The group wanted to include environment and carbon targets into the contract to help with its corporate objectives. Having asked the question 'How does it work now?', it turned out there was no process or approach for carbon savings. However, it was pointed out that there was a huge wind turbine on the roof, which hadn't got there by accident. Two weeks later the team had produced a process flowchart that illustrated how things currently worked. As a result they had spotted that they were paying **two** suppliers to provide them with the same services, providing them with an immediate benefit, before they had actually changed anything.

The next example is a more complex one for a call centre providing technical support. Figure 5.4 shows a detailed model of how the service worked. It provides a much clearer illustration of the potential

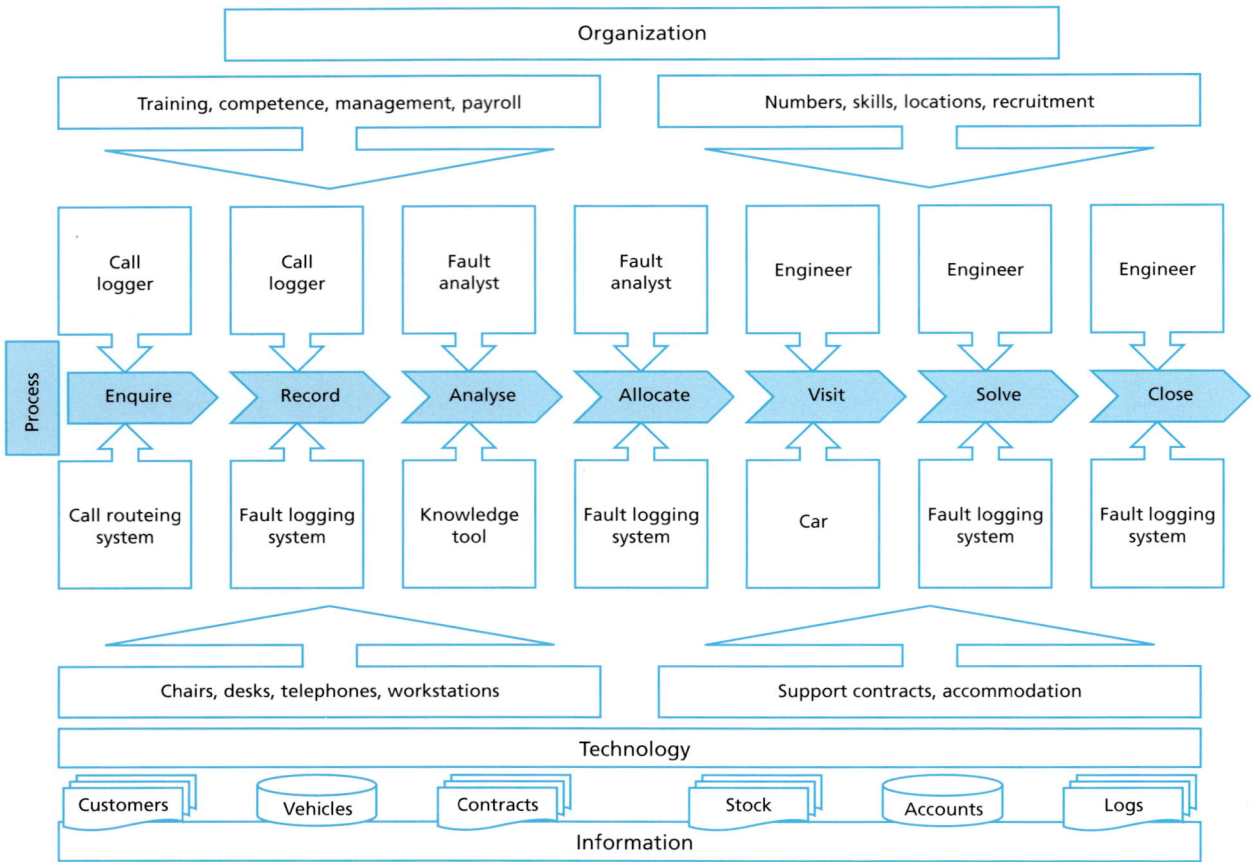

Figure 5.4 Example of a detailed POTI model

effects of a restructure and helped the organization understand where they needed to invest training and where the risks lay.

You will note that Figure 5.4 still uses the POTI headings but in a way that is easier to understand.

When developing the 'as-is' state, always focus on the service and then the process because the technology and people revolve around them, as does the management information.

5.3.4 How will it work in the future?

The challenge in producing the future state is that the vision statement may not be specific or adequate to enable this to happen. Vision statements are often a compromise that has been agreed to by all parties because they can interpret it differently for their own audiences; consequently, it becomes management waffle.

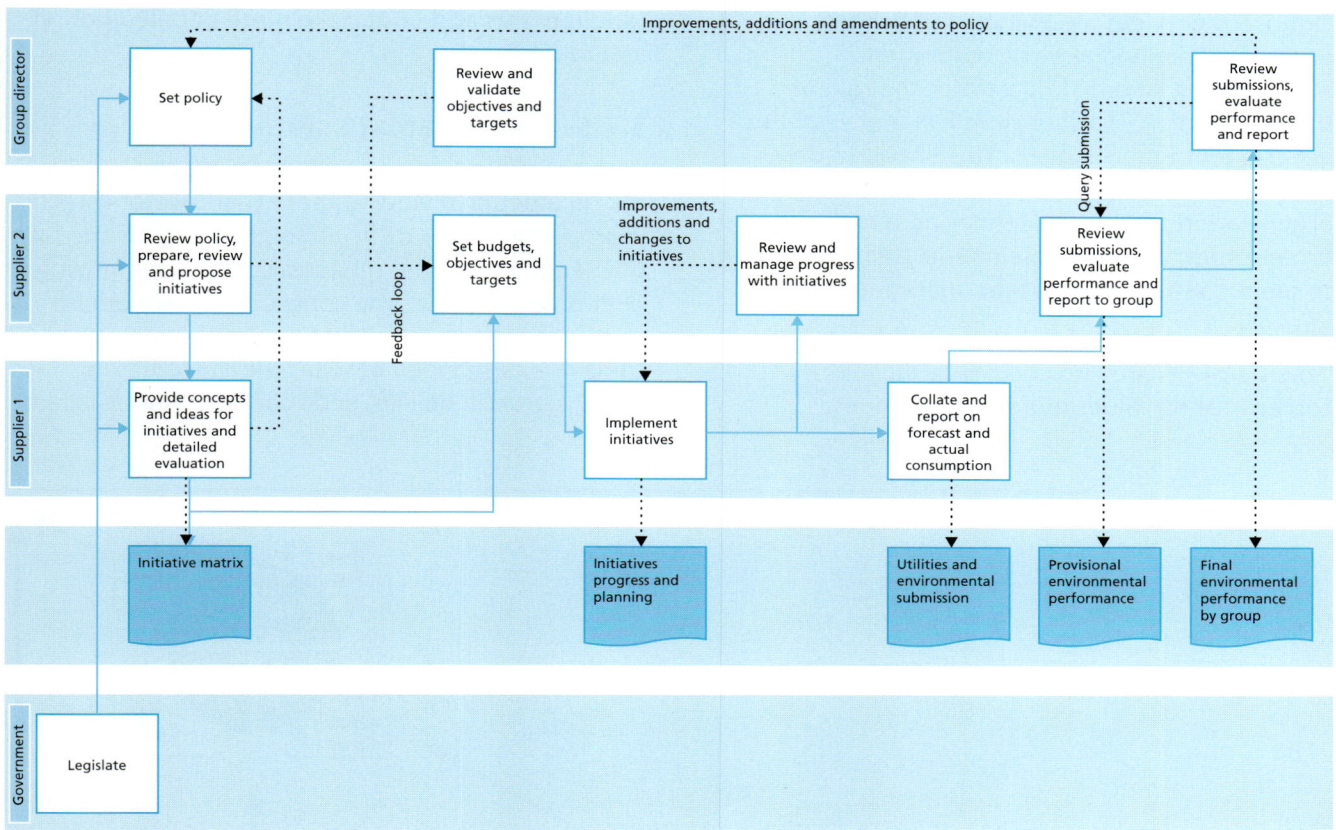

Figure 5.5 Overview of an environmental management system

Developing a blueprint from management waffle or a vision statement that has managed to avoid any clear statements of intent is going to be a bit tricky and this is the problem many programmes have.

The advice on putting the blueprint together now applies to the future state, and the starting point is to ask the following questions:

- What services will be changed, stopped or started?
- What will be the impact of this on the way you operate?
- What structural changes to the organization, market and supply chain will be needed?
- What technology, infrastructure, legislation or property changes are anticipated?
- What information will you need to manage this and where will it come from?

All this information can be captured in simple process flowcharts or cross-functional flowchart diagrams. These are relatively easy to create, easy to understand and can contain all the necessary detail for decision-making.

Figure 5.5 provides an overview of how an organization managed its environmental management system. It illustrates the role of the organization, various suppliers and even the government in the process. This provided the basis for developing the specification that the organization used for its tendering process; the organization was also able to analyse responses to see the effect on its target operating model/blueprint.

When projects are launched, they will use the contents of the blueprint as their business

requirements and undertake more detailed design at a lower level.

5.3.5 Intermediate states

As many programmes have a long life expectancy, taking a detailed view of more than two or three years ahead is very difficult and pointless as the rate of change means the goalposts are always moving. That is why MSP has the concept of intermediate states (see Figure 5.6). This enables the programme to have a rough idea of what the outcomes in eight years will be like, and then do more detailed

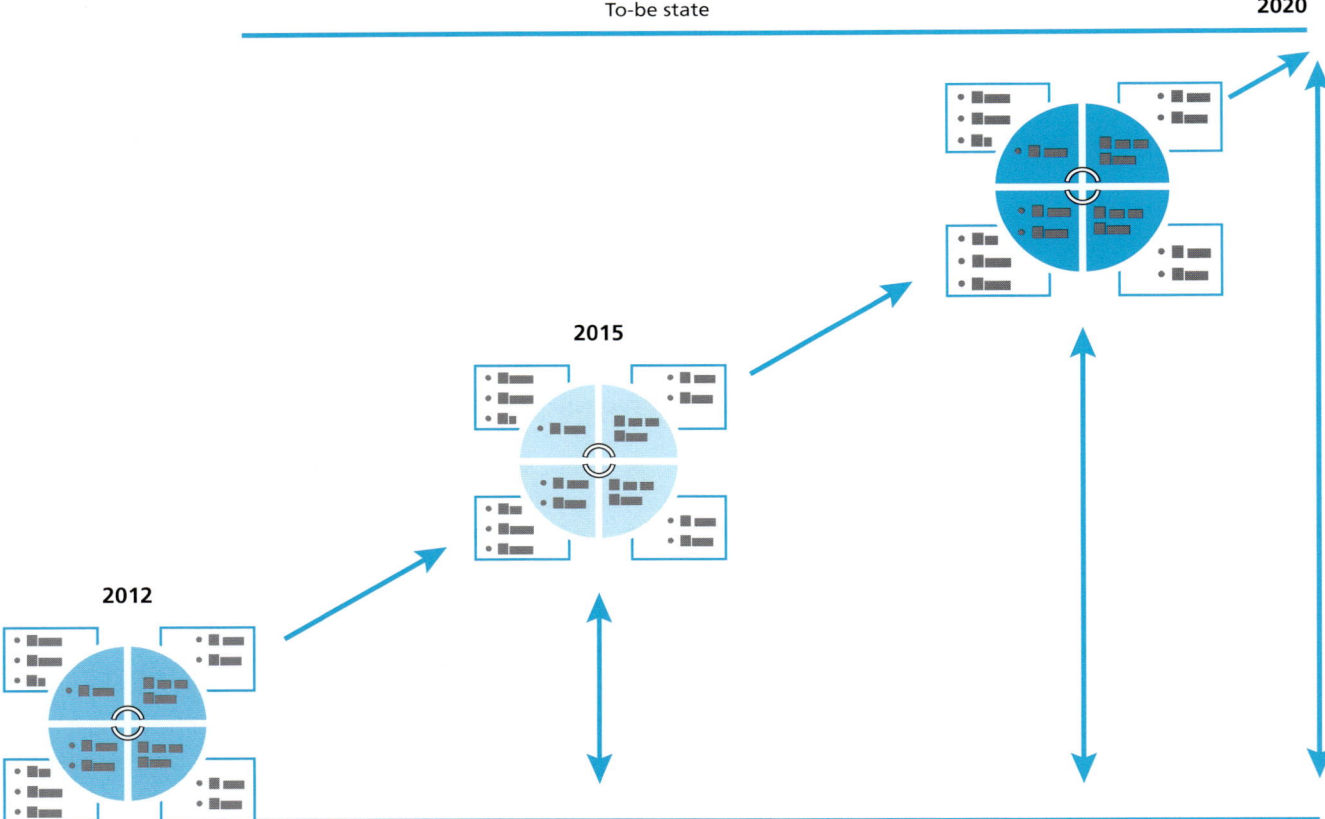

Figure 5.6 Programme intermediate state

thinking against a more reasonable planning horizon (e.g. three years).

Intermediate states are also useful if there is a lot of ambiguity in the environment, which could be driven by markets, politics or technological dynamics.

Intermediate states provide the basis for decisions and changes of direction to the programme and provide the detail that is needed for project initiation and benefits forecasting. You will therefore find them useful as you try to develop the definition of what the future will be like.

Intermediate states provide you with foreseeable targets.

Within MSP the concept of a tranche is linked to intermediate blueprints, as each tranche delivers a step change in capability.

Hints and tips

The TOGAF model (The Open Group, 2011) for developing organizational architectures is a valuable framework within which a number of organizational or sector blueprints can be developed to a common standard.

5.3.6   What are the challenges you face?

There are a number of challenges that you will face during the development of the blueprint. These can be regarded as risks for the programme and you may wish to have them logged formally so that they are visible to everyone.

Many organizations have found that they often do have blueprint information, but it is dispersed around a number of documents. During investigation it often becomes apparent that work has already taken place to develop some aspect of the blueprint and it is gathering dust somewhere or is embedded in disparate places, so part of the work at this stage is finding the information and assembling it. The strategic business plan is often a good place to start, as the programme is almost certainly linked to a strategic objective of some sort.

Example

Some early blueprint work with a programme that had become a little becalmed happened to unearth the organization's three-year business plan. The document was a very aspirational and optimistic view of what their world would be like in three years' time, as expressed by each of the directors. It wasn't anything like a plan, but it was a very detailed vision statement that provided a good starting point for developing the blueprint. The document was used to run workshops to answer the question: 'What needs to be in place to enable your objectives?', and subsequently led to the outline blueprint for each area being changed.

It would be good to be able to make this easy for you, but the truth is that it isn't easy. The process will find problems in many programmes that people want to avoid, but all this avoidance achieves is postponing problems that are coming anyway.

Where an issue with the blueprint cannot be resolved, it should be logged as an issue formally within the programme to ensure that it is dealt with by the programme board or escalated to the sponsoring group.

The challenges that you may face, include:

- Difficulty in finding people who know how the systems actually work

- Gaps between how the systems should work and how they actually work
- Getting decisions made about the level of change that is acceptable
- Conflicting priorities from different groups leading to different requirements
- Disagreements between BCMs on the way forward
- Lack of strategic commitment to the level of necessary change
- Existing projects that are not aligned with what is needed but nobody has the will to stop them
- Finding the right resources and expertise to do the work
- Confidentiality, as some of the issues that arise may be very sensitive, particularly in terms of industrial relations and the press.

Some ideas on how these challenges can be addressed include using:

- Workshops to get people involved (but ensure they are properly briefed)
- Targeted questionnaires to gather views and details on how things currently function and how they could be improved
- Quality management systems
- Existing strategies that set out how things may work (e.g. ICT or property)
- Handbooks and guidelines that set out how operations work.

5.3.7 Business architecture

The term 'business architecture' refers to the architectural organization of an enterprise or a business unit. A formal definition by the Object Management Group that very much aligns with the MSP perspective is as follows:

'A blueprint of the enterprise that provides a common understanding of the organization and is used to align strategic objectives and tactical demands.'

Business architecture is now a well-developed concept and works on the same principles as a blueprint in MSP, but is far more developed as a methodology in terms of its vocabulary, structure and supporting techniques. People who build business architectures are known as business architects, and they are particularly valuable if you are working in an organization with multiple programmes. Business architecture provides a common framework on which to build the programme blueprints and enables cross-referencing and interdependencies to be managed on more than one level. Its disciplined approach will help you to realize business models that enhance accountability and improve your decision-making.

Business architecture's value proposition, unlike other disciplines, is to increase functional effectiveness by mapping and modelling the business to its vision and strategic goals. It does this by:

- Identifying gaps between the current architectural state and target state (mapping)
- Discovering business requirements in the area of interest, including stakeholders, business entities and their relationships, and business integration points (modelling).

In order to develop an integrated view of the business, many different views are typically developed. The key views within the business architecture are:

- **Business strategy view** Describes the strategic goals that energize an organization and give it purpose. The goals may be expressed as various tactical approaches that can be traced through the business. They are mapped to metrics to provide an ongoing evaluation of how well the business is doing. The goals also contribute to benefits.

- **Business capabilities view** Describes the business's functional abilities. This view further distinguishes between functions that are customer-facing, supplier-related, core business executive or related to business management. This view contributes to identifying the projects and capabilities that the business must deliver to achieve the target state.

- **Business knowledge view** Establishes the shared semantics (e.g. customer, order and supplier) within an organization and the relationships between them (e.g. customer name, order date, supplier name). These semantics form the vocabulary that the business relies upon to communicate and structure the areas it operates within.

- **Business operational view** Defines the set of structures that transcend functional and organizational boundaries. It also sets the boundary of the organization by identifying and describing external entities such as customers, suppliers and external systems that interact with the business.

- **Organizational view** Describes the relationships between roles, capabilities and business units, the breakdown of those business units into subunits, and the internal or external management of those units.

In addition to these views of the business, the relationships connecting them form the foundation of the programme blueprint and provide diagnostic evidence to develop the benefits and identify the projects needed to achieve the capabilities and outcomes.

There are a number of models and techniques that have been developed under the discipline of business architecture, any of which will provide you with helpful suggestions for developing your blueprint. It is too big a topic to cover in this publication, but this section should have given you a taster.

5.3.8 What happens if you don't have a blueprint?

The consequences of not having a blueprint are often not immediately apparent to a programme. Hopefully, there will be a vision and the programme will set off launching projects that will provide the energy to take the programme to the perceived destination. This happy state can last for up to a year, sometimes more. The organization will be pleased about the apparent progress and the programme team will be motivated and energized by delivering projects and reporting on their progress.

The problems usually begin to emerge at between 6 and 12 months. The programme will appear disengaged from the organization that it is changing, because it has little understanding of the organization that it is planning to change. The programme board will be focused on project delivery, and if it did manage to appoint business change managers their role will be rather vague and ambiguous.

Decision-making, which was fast and energetic in the early days, will become slower and problems more complex. Priorities and the basis for decisions will be unclear, momentum will be lost and the programme will appear to become becalmed.

This is not always a bad thing to happen, as it is a chance to regroup, celebrate the apparent successes, consider where the programme is going and put appropriate controls in place. Many programmes experience this stage and, by using the MSP framework as a point of reference, the programme has achieved the first step change in capability, as it has realized that delivering a programme through project techniques and lots of energy is not enough.

This isn't always what happens. For example, programmes that are short term (often compliance programmes) where there are big targets to hit with hard deadlines, can be successful in forcing a change through. The test of whether it was a true programme is whether the change sticks and the benefits come from the investment.

5.4 YOUR ROLE IN DEVELOPING THE VISION AND BLUEPRINT

The BCM is not alone in developing the vision and blueprint, but the result of the work is going to shape your role for the life of the programme and the destiny of the organization.

5.4.1 Other BCMs

You will need to work closely with the other BCMs: conflicts are inevitable over the structure of the future organization, which may shape people's power bases once the programme is over and will colour their contributions. If the problems cannot be resolved at the programme board then the sponsoring group will need to be engaged.

5.4.2 Programme manager

The programme manager has responsibility for the actual blueprint document, as it is a core part of the programme controls, and the projects will be initiated to create the capability that is described in the blueprint. Therefore, if the blueprint does not exist or is incomplete, the wrong projects may be launched. The programme manager should be pushing to get the job done and should provide help and experience where appropriate, although the content must be owned by the BCMs.

5.4.3 The senior responsible owner

Ultimately, the SRO is accountable for what the programme produces and must sign off the blueprint. The SRO should be heavily engaged in the process and should provide advice and direction to resolve strategic or tactical issues quickly. The SRO is also the conduit to the sponsoring group and should refer upwards, as appropriate, any conflicts that cannot be resolved.

Table 5.2 is from the MSP guide and sets out the specific areas of focus for each role in developing the vision and blueprint.

Table 5.2 Key roles in blueprint design and delivery

Role	Area of focus
Senior responsible owner (SRO)	Providing strategic direction for the work of the design of the blueprint and analysis of delivery options
	Ensuring sponsoring group authorization and commitment to the 'to-be' state, demonstrated through active cooperation; for example, making appropriate resource available to assist with the design of the blueprint and analysis of delivery options
	Ensuring that the blueprint document remains aligned with the strategic direction of the organization and will promote a coherent capability
	Providing the interface to the sponsoring group and other key stakeholders, maintaining their buy-in; for example, as the design of the future organization becomes clearer
	Providing advice and direction to the programme manager and BCM(s) as required, including risks or issues identified during blueprint design and delivery
	Ensuring that the programme board assesses and understands the implications of the blueprint and its delivery
Programme manager	Ensuring that the blueprint document is authored and assembled in collaboration with the BCM(s)
	Working closely with the BCM(s) to ensure that the blueprint, programme plan, benefits realization plan and benefit profiles are consistent and able to deliver the business case
	Ensuring the programme has access to competent resources to create the blueprint
	Ensuring that appropriate options appraisals to select the optimal 'to-be' state take place
	Ensuring that the management of changes is undertaken with an impact assessment on the blueprint
	Communicating the details of the blueprint to the relevant projects and other programmes
	Ensuring that the planned step changes in operational capability are clearly understood by the project teams
	Ensuring that uncertainties and ambiguities relating to the content of the blueprint are captured as risks
	Contributing to managing stakeholder expectations

Table continues

Table 5.2 *continued*

Role	Area of focus
Business change manager(s)	Leading the development of the content and taking responsibility for the delivery of the design into business operations
	Consulting with and gaining support from senior business managers for the 'to-be' state
	Ensuring that the planned step changes in operational capability are clearly understood by the operational areas
	Providing and coordinating essential input to the blueprint with the assistance of experienced operational staff and specialists, and (where appropriate) authoring (at least part of) the blueprint
	Ensuring that 'as-is' and 'to-be' information from the blueprint is used to construct the benefit profiles
	Aligning the creation of the capability within the blueprint with benefits realization through approval of project outputs
	Ensuring that operational changes during the life of the programme are being reflected in the evolving 'as-is' state in the blueprint
Programme office	Providing or locating information and resources that can assist with the design of the blueprint
	Facilitating impact assessments of changes on the blueprint
	Maintaining configuration control of the blueprint

Benefits management

6

6 Benefits management

'There is nothing more difficult to take in hand, more perilous to conduct, or more uncertain in its success, than to take the lead in the introduction of a new order of things.'
Niccolò Machiavelli

For you as the business change manager (BCM) benefits management is your primary focus. The role exists to deliver change, either internally or externally of the organization. Benefits are the justification for this change and they can come in many shapes, sizes and forms.

Research by KPMG in 2006 suggested that less than 80% of predicted benefits were delivered in the average project. Analysis of the result of the P3M3 (Portfolio, Programme and Project Management Maturity Model) assessments in 2010 by Aspire Europe showed that 90% of organizations were at Level 1 maturity for benefits management. This means that there were no formal processes or plans in place to deliver benefits for the vast majority of initiatives, which supported the conclusions of KPMG and showed that little had changed in the four years in between. By 2014, however, the impact of MSP and the recession had increased focus on achieving value for money. Further analysis of P3M3 results showed a noticeable improvement in benefits management, with 50% of organizations achieving Level 2 and a number achieving Level 3.

The reality of the situation is that most investments and programmes do achieve positive results. The problem is that programmes do not focus enough on benefits and do little to track or record them, so there is no evidence they were achieved. This is due largely to the lack of good-quality BCMs operating within programme structures who fully understand their role. Hopefully this publication is going to change all that!

There are numerous publications on benefits management that can go into far more detail than this one can, for example *Managing Benefits* by Steve Jenner (2012), *Fundamentals of Benefit Realization* by Gerald Bradley (2010) and of course the MSP guide itself. This publication will focus on the role of the BCM and benefits rather than generic benefits management theory.

6.1 BASIC PRINCIPLES

Benefits are the positive effects of change. Within the programme the change that is required is defined in the blueprint; therefore, there is an inherent link between the blueprint and the benefits.

The blueprint describes what the current state is, what the future state will be and the benefits that will result from the change. So, if insufficient effort is invested in developing a detailed understanding for the blueprint, then the basis for estimating benefits will be flawed and, in effect, the benefits will be guesswork – and, in most cases, bad guesses.

Figure 5.6 in Chapter 5 shows how the achievement of intermediate states in the blueprint can give the opportunity to release and measure benefits after step changes in capability.

The problem with programmes is they tend to put all their focus on the cost of creating the change rather than the beneficial effects of the change.

The type of programme will significantly affect the approach to benefits:

- **Vision-led programmes** will be the most benefits-focused. By their nature they are higher risk and, as such, the anticipated rewards will be expected to be higher, so the analysis to validate the potential benefits from the change is likely to have a higher level of focus.
- **Emergent programmes** may initially be focused on the added value from optimizing the delivery of projects; however, the benefits should appear from the aggregated value of the benefits from the various initiatives. Quite often there are initiatives that are struggling to justify themselves as stand-alone projects, but when constituted as a programme the potential to provide benefits is much greater.

Example

An IT call centre rationalization included a number of upgrade projects which were needed but were difficult to justify. By raising the bar and combining them as a programme with a more ambitious rationalization of the processes and structures based on the combined effect of the new technology, the programme business case was much easier to sell.

- **Compliance programmes** are often the most difficult to develop the benefits for. This is because there is little or no choice about the changes that have to be made, only the level of ambition. These programmes can be driven by legislative changes like carbon emissions, market changes or, in the public sector, implementing

political changes that are based on philosophy rather than benefits. In these situations, the benefits are often the avoidance of the consequences of not taking action, and they may well not match the cost of the programme at all.

The following sections describe the guiding principles for effective benefits management.

6.1.1 Establish the guiding mind

There must be a single point of focus in the organization for benefits delivery. This can be an individual at the top of the organization (in the same way that there is a finance director) who is taking personal responsibility for the delivery of the change; for example, the senior responsible owner (SRO) within the programme.

There is also a need for some form of subject matter expert who supports the BCMs, sometimes called a benefits realization manager, who will be the person that advises and provides assurance on benefits realization plans and profiles.

Example

An organization established a benefits realization board to take a view across all the programmes. Programmes only had to report by exception if they were not going to deliver the benefits, which put the onus on them to be transparent about the reality of the situation: a reverse psychology was in action. Those that didn't report were assumed to be on schedule but were often subject to audits, so it was easier to report concerns than hide them away and certainly better for people's career potentials.

Too often reports on benefits are excessively optimistic and not based on the reality of the change. When a group only has one focus, such as benefits, it will be very single minded. The BCMs could provide a 'guiding mind' for the programme as a collective.

This 'guiding mind' can then also deal with double-counting of benefits or where programmes and/or projects are affecting the same performance indicators to help with primary ownership and resolve any conflicts that may arise.

6.1.2 Transparent and tangible evidence base

Benefits forecasts must be evidence based rather than guesswork. This will require measurement of current performance to establish a baseline and the metrics to assess improvements. The relevant metrics will be monitored to validate any estimates, opportunities and threats that may develop.

Each change must clearly define how a benefit's achievement can be audited and viewed once the change has been delivered, with evidence to support that claim of achievement.

6.1.3 Attribution for achievement

There will be clear accountability for each benefit, and elements of that benefit will be signed up to by the appropriate department representative. The responsibilities and activities for delivering the business changes that will realize the benefits should be clearly defined in the benefits documentation and used for tracking and auditing the delivery.

The delivery of a benefit should be allocated to individuals with, most importantly, a single point of accountability. The expectations and responsibilities for these individuals should be clearly defined and

where possible formally contracted. The BCM may not have direct control of all aspects of benefits but can use this technique to get others signed up to the change.

6.1.4 Risk-based valuation

No benefit is certain; it will most likely be dependent on a number of inputs which will need to be effectively managed to achieve the values that have been forecast.

It is essential to understand the level of risk associated with the achievement of the benefit, as this contributes to understanding the overall level of risk for the programme. The best way to manage the benefit risk is to associate a numeric value with the level of risk and use this to factor the amount of the benefit that is achievable.

For example, numeric levels could be applied to individual benefits as follows:

- Low risk = 90% of the value is achievable
- Medium risk = 60% of the value is achievable
- High risk = 30% of the value is achievable.

If a benefit has been identified that is worth £100,000, but there are a number of risks associated with it and its likelihood of being achieved is medium, you might only account for £60,000 in the benefits forecast, as this is the most likely benefit realization. If effort is put into removing the risks then the £100,000 would still be achievable. This helps to reflect the uncertainty associated with benefits and create more accurate forecasts.

6.1.5 Control of change

A major threat to any benefit is the failure to control organizational changes or reflect changing market conditions. Failure to realize a benefit can be caused inadvertently by programme or project boards or operations making scope or process changes without understanding the impact.

Once a benefit has been identified, none of the elements that contribute to the value should be changed, re-invested or re-utilized without change control being applied and formal approval. The 'guiding mind' is crucial to maintaining focus and resolving conflicts.

To maintain focus, all programme and project boards must have benefits as a standing item on their agenda.

Hints and tips

There is a very simple way of dealing with internal cost saving measures: when the business case is approved, simply go to the financial plan and remove the budgeted amount from the cost centre in the forecast year. This is the ultimate form of benefits harvesting and ensures they are delivered.

Benefits harvesting has been deployed in a number of organizations since 2010 when UK public sector cost-cutting started. It tends to happen in organizations that are using portfolio management approaches where there is stronger management control of change.

6.1.6 Consistent valuations

To enable consistent and effective comparison of proposals for change, and to enable a common 'currency' for approving, reporting and releasing benefits, it is essential that there is consistency of valuation.

There needs to be a framework that defines what are acceptable valuations and criteria. These are the only ones that will be accepted when the change is proposed. This will enable consistent accounting for benefits against these criteria.

Ideally, all calculations will be financially valued, but clarity will be sought as to whether each benefit is cashable or not. The use of monetary value enables the lowest common denominator for comparison.

The cost of achieving the benefit must be included in the calculation; a profile of anticipated costs will be used as part of the benefit profiles, and be tracked to ensure that the balance between cost and return is maintained.

6.2 WHAT DOES MSP HAVE TO SAY?

Benefits management is at the very heart of programme management: programmes are primarily driven by the need to deliver benefits. This is achieved by the programme's projects creating outputs, which build capabilities, which in turn transition into outcomes that serve the purpose of realizing benefits for the organization. However, it is likely that the programme will have some negative impacts as well as improvements.

Where a negative effect of the change can be forecast, then this is termed a dis-benefit. Benefits and dis-benefits can be defined as follows:

- A **benefit** is the measurable improvement resulting from an outcome perceived as an advantage by one or more stakeholders, which contributes towards one or more organizational objective(s).
- A **dis-benefit** is the measurable decline resulting from an outcome perceived as negative by one or more stakeholders, which detracts from one or more organizational objective(s).

Understanding the differences and relationships between outputs, capabilities, outcomes and benefits is key to understanding benefits management (see Table 6.1).

Given its importance to the programme, it is not surprising that benefits management drives many aspects of programme management including:

■ Aligning and validating the integrity of the blueprint against the projects, activities and associated organizational changes needed to deliver the new capabilities and benefits

■ Defining the aggregate of achieved benefits, expected benefits, costs to date and expected cost against the business case; providing a crucial test of the ongoing viability of the programme

■ Prioritizing benefits to allow the programme to create maximum value under given constraints and make the right trade-off decisions if required

■ Planning the programme (benefits realization is a major foundation for this aspect)

■ Engaging with stakeholders to understand impact and helping win support

■ Defining what is a fit-for-purpose capability, establishing what the critical quality-checking mechanisms throughout the programme would be and checking that they are aligned with the requirements in the blueprint

Table 6.1 Differences between outputs, capabilities, outcomes and benefits

	Output	Capability	Outcome	Benefit
Description	The deliverable, or output developed by a project from a planned activity	The completed set of project outputs required to deliver an outcome; exists prior to transition	A new operational state achieved after transition of the capability into live operations	The measurable improvement resulting from an outcome perceived as an advantage by one or more stakeholders and which contributes towards one or more organizational objective(s)
Rationale	Answers at least in part the fundamental question 'What do you need to create to enable the change?'	Answers the question 'What will you need to have in place to enable the new operating state?'	Answers the question 'What is the desired operational state of the organization using these new things?'	Answers the question 'Why is this justified?' (i.e. it explains what a programme delivers)
Example	An individual component of an e-commerce system, application, hardware, new business processes training etc.	An e-commerce system tested and ready to go into operation and with trained staff	Transformed client service organization, faster processing, fulfilling and charging for web-based orders	Increased sales revenues of x%

- Informing end-of-tranche reviews to enable decisions on changes to the programme going forward and underlying governance to be made
- Ensuring that the costs associated with Delivering the Capability are balanced with the value of the benefits in the business case
- Monitoring the risks and issues that may impact benefits realization.

6.2.1 Benefits categorization

Categorizing benefits can help organizations to better model their priorities and planning and ensure that there is a balanced portfolio of benefits. By categorizing benefits effectively, organizations are able to:

- Balance the mix of benefits that are being sought and the associated risk profiles
- Enable effective reporting and tracking by category
- Identify potential overlaps of benefit counting
- Understand the impact of changes on different parts of the organization
- Track the relationship between objectives and benefits
- Help to manage changes to priorities within the programmes. If there is a strategic change in the value types being sought, the programme will be more agile in its ability to see the impact across the programme
- Help to create a common set of terminology for referring to benefits and bring greater transparency
- Enable a portfolio-level view of benefits across programmes and projects through consistency.

There are many different ways to categorize benefits. The following benefit categories are well established, but they are not exhaustive:

- Value
- Financial impact
- Corporate objective
- Stakeholder impact
- Timeline
- Levels of risk.

6.3 WHAT DOES THIS MEAN TO YOU?

6.3.1 The benefits cycle and techniques

'If you want to make enemies, try to change something.' Woodrow Wilson

As with most of the themes in MSP, there is a cycle of activities that run throughout the programme and it is your job to manage this cycle and ensure that it happens.

Figure 3.1 in Chapter 3 shows a typical theme lifecycle and illustrates the four steps that cover the evolution of benefits and their maintenance.

6.3.1.1 Identify

Identification begins right at the start of the programme. In fact it may start pre-programme when the strategy is being developed and the benefits are first identified. The starting point for the benefits hunt is:

- **Corporate objectives** Alignment and contribution to the achievement of the organization's objectives (see, for example, Table 6.2)
- **Internal sources** Improvements internal to the organization
- **External sources** Improvements delivered to the supply chain, economy or consumers.

Table 6.2 Corporate objectives

Objective	High-level description
Process rationalization	Changes to any business process that creates an improvement in or reduces the steps and associated costs of delivering a service
Staff utilization	Fewer people being deployed to achieve a task or the resources being used in a different way that enables a measurable improvement
Supply chain rationalization	Reduction in supply chain complexity or opening up the supply market to increase competition will provide a justification for investment as long as the value can be measured
Improved control	Better management information that reduces the analysis or increases the availability of knowledge will contribute to more effective decision-making and better control
Asset utilization	Better use of the property, technology or production asset base by reduction or increased utilization
Reduced organizational risk	An investment that reduces or removes a threat. This could reduce the costs that are in place as contingency for dealing with the consequences, should the threat occur
Customer satisfaction	Increases loyalty, which potentially offers benefits in avoidance of costs for acquiring new customers
Brand enhancement	Reduces negative media interest or increases customer loyalty on which benefits can be built

The reason that the programme is initiated will often affect the types of benefit that can be pursued. If the programme is fundamentally compliance in nature and doing nothing is not an option, then the benefits may well be found in the avoidance of the negative consequences that would have resulted from doing nothing.

Internal benefits are derived from making changes to the ways of working that release benefits into the operations. Whether these are harvested as an economic, efficiency or effectiveness benefit will depend on the opportunities and priorities for the business at that time.

You will note that many of these terms are what you may have actually called benefits, but they are not. They are basically capabilities, objectives or maybe outcomes that the programme will produce. You will be exploiting them.

Table 6.3 is more applicable to public sector organizations, where the investment is often related to the beneficial effect that it will have on society.

Identification is the step when you will normally create your initial benefits map to show what the programme will deliver so that there is an illustration of the cause and effect between the capability that is being produced and the benefits that are being forecast.

Table 6.3 Example public sector objectives

Objective	High-level summary
Market management	Levels of investment by private sector
	Levels of competition
	Confidence of market participants
	Reduced use of levies
	Liquidity measures = number of trades
Improved community safety	A change that provides greater safety to members of the local community or members of the public
Protection for the vulnerable	Will provide greater security to vulnerable groups within the community through improved care, environment or monitoring
Enhanced community amenities	Will provide more or improved local amenities to a region in terms of services and built environment
Improved transport	The change will improve the transportation links in a region or within certain specific areas
Improved economy	The change will improve the economic performance of a region, which will attract more businesses into the area, reduce unemployment and increase citizens' wealth
Fit-for-purpose services	Ensuring appropriate service levels are in place to meet local customer needs while achieving any legislative obligations or imposed criteria

6.3.1.2 Analyse and profile

Once the potential benefits have been identified they need to be systematically analysed to calculate their financial value, identify changes that need to happen to enable their delivery and establish the level of risk associated with the calculations.

This work should be done in collaboration with the creation of the blueprint, as the capability being designed will need to deliver the changes that you need in order to achieve the benefits.

This is the step during which you would normally develop your benefits management strategy and create your benefit profiles that will underpin the business case.

Financial impact

It is much better if a benefit has a financial value allocated to it and it is important to be clear as to whether the achievement of this value is cashable or not. Failure to be clear on this is often the cause of lost or misunderstood benefits and the blame game will begin. In this context:

■ **Cashable** benefits are those where the money is released by the organization to reduce costs or for further investment.

■ **Non-cashable** benefits are where an efficiency saving is achieved across a number of activities and provides the potential to do more, but no cash is released. This is often associated with full-time equivalents savings where there is the potential to do more, but there is a danger that the saving is absorbed back into the organization and the benefit is not delivered.

Both cashable and non-cashable benefits can be measured in financial terms, but understanding the difference is important where cost savings are required to be delivered; non-cashable benefits are of very little use for this.

Value types

It is important to note that for any particular change initiative there may be positive values against one value type, but with a negative impact on one of the other sources. For example, you might make an efficiency improvement but with a deterioration in service levels. Both measures need to be captured to enable the right management decisions to be made.

Table 6.4 describes the three value types.

The value types are really helpful in finding benefits and tracking them during the programme and they

Table 6.4 The three value types

Category	Description
Economic	Improvements that generate: ■ Better cash flow ■ More income ■ Lower costs ■ Better capital utilization.
Efficiency	An efficiency is only a benefit if the resources are released to do other work or are no longer in place. Improvements that create an efficiency are: ■ Achieving the same level of service with less resources ■ Delivering more services with the same resources.
Effectiveness	Improvements that create effectiveness are: ■ Fewer failures or complaints ■ Increased customer satisfaction ■ Higher quality of service ■ Better management control or flexibility ■ Improved legislative compliance ■ Better service resilience.

Table 6.5 Internal example

Capability/value type	Economic measures	Efficiency measures	Effectiveness measures
Process improvement	£x saved on external support This will be visible in the following budget lines: xxx	xxx fewer FTEs used to achieve the process The posts involved will be xxxx and their duties will no longer involve yyyy	£x saved in reduced failures of installation, which currently run at £xxx per month The cost of these failures is £y, and these costs will be removed from budget line nn

Table 6.6 Benefit value categories

Benefit category/value type	Economic measures	Efficiency measures	Effectiveness measures
More renewable energy production	More jobs in the energy generation industry	Reduction in the resources used to reduce overall emissions	Reduced dependency on carbon generation technology

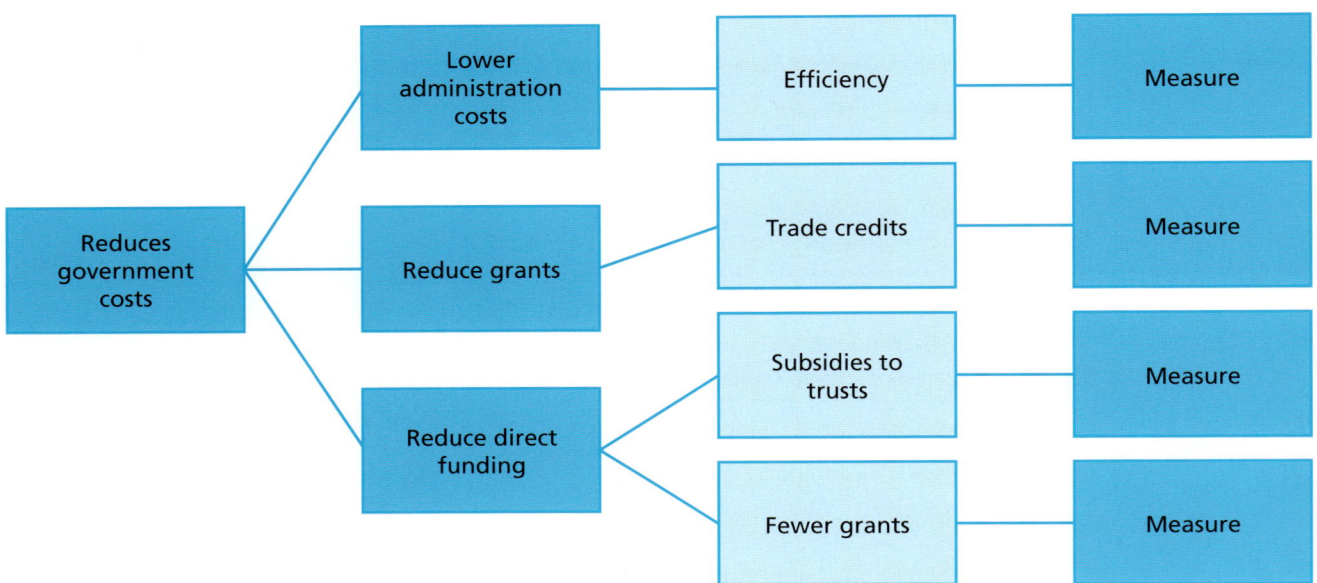

Figure 6.1 Example of a benefits map in reverse order

also help to show how a new capability will have positive and negative effects.

The benefits can be illustrated against each value type. A simple example for an internal benefit is shown in Table 6.5. It helps to show that you can only improve a process so far before it deteriorates, rather like stretching an elastic band.

In the example shown in Table 6.5, the capability is process improvement. As you reduce the number of people involved, you can release external support to give better cash flow. You can release internal resources involved with the process and, up to a certain point, the quality of service could improve, or at least not deteriorate. However, there will come a point where the effectiveness will drop as resources are reduced; this could be through slower response time or more errors being made.

Table 6.6 shows how a benefit category such as more renewable energy production can achieve measurable improvements across the three benefit value types.

6.3.1.3 Measure and plan

There are two ways to plan. The normal approach is to start at the beginning and work forward, but one of the problems is that the timing of the end may not fit with the strategic needs of the programme. The alternative is to start at the end and work backwards so that you can work out what needs to be done by when.

Figure 6.1 shows a benefits map in reverse order, which some people find easier to deal with. It shows how a government might try to reduce costs.

Benefits must be consistently measured and tracked to show where and how the benefit will manifest itself. The first thing to work out is what you will measure and the second is when the measurable improvements will occur. Table 6.7 shows some examples of measurement headings.

Planning for benefits achievement is inherently linked to delivery of the blueprint by the projects. The focus of planning for the BCM is about creating the readiness for the organization to change, managing it through that cycle and releasing the benefits.

A key part of planning is projecting the effects of the change on performance, putting in place contingency plans to cope with any potential deterioration in performance, and forecasting when and where the improvements will occur.

The timeline categorization (section 6.2.1) can be used as part of planning, to show when groups of benefits will be released and their value. This will enable prioritization of different types of benefits to be released, particularly if cashable benefits are needed to fund further tranches of the programme.

This is covered in more detail in Part 3 of this publication on the transformational flow processes, which looks at the steps in the change and how you fit into this.

6.3.1.4 Deliver and review

Implementation is directly linked to the delivery of the blueprint. The projects will be creating the capability for you, so you will need to be focused on when and where this will occur and what you need to do to make the change happen.

As part of measurement you will have identified what the performance levels are on the indicators that you have chosen. This information should have been stored in the blueprint and/or the benefit profiles.

Table 6.7 Benefit measurement headings

Measurement	Description
Cash saving	Cashable reduction in the cost as a result of making the change
	The amount of the saving must be attributable to a financial budget and be approved by the financial partner
FTE reduction	Fewer people used to deliver the service. These people can then be released or re-deployed
	The posts that will be affected must be identified, with specific reference to what activities will not now be undertaken, and how the released effort will be used
Reduced transaction time	Time it takes to deliver a service, either internal or externally. The time that is saved can then be turned into a measurable value
	This must be illustrated with specific reference to the tasks that are no longer required, or the obstacle that is being removed which will enable the speeding up of the transaction
Reduced failure rate	Service or product failures that are removed and the associated value of failures that are being avoided
	This must be illustrated by analysis of the root cause of the failures and the impacts of these failures that justify their removal
Organizational performance indicators	Contributes to a change in an identified indicator, which in itself must have a measurable value to the organization, in particular if that indicator supports a strategic objective
	The specific indicator must be defined, and an explanation given of how the indicator will be changed, and what the benefit of changing this indicator is
Customer satisfaction	Improvement in the satisfaction of the consumers of the service by a measurable amount. This measurable amount must be attributable to the planned change
	There must be a description of the current levels of satisfaction, how this was measured, the level of change that is anticipated, and how this improvement will be measured

The target performance levels, once the programme has completed, will also have been estimated, as these will be the basis for the benefit calculations.

As the programme moves through delivery, maintaining a track of the anticipated performance levels against what was predicted is essential and part of the BCM role (see Figure 6.2). After initial implementation the performance is likely to be volatile, which is why you need time to allow the performance to stabilize before the benefits can be claimed.

Throughout this process lessons are going to be learned that will need to be factored into future benefits planning. Some areas that will require monitoring, review and probably improvement include:

■ Suitability of the measure
■ Accuracy and availability of the information

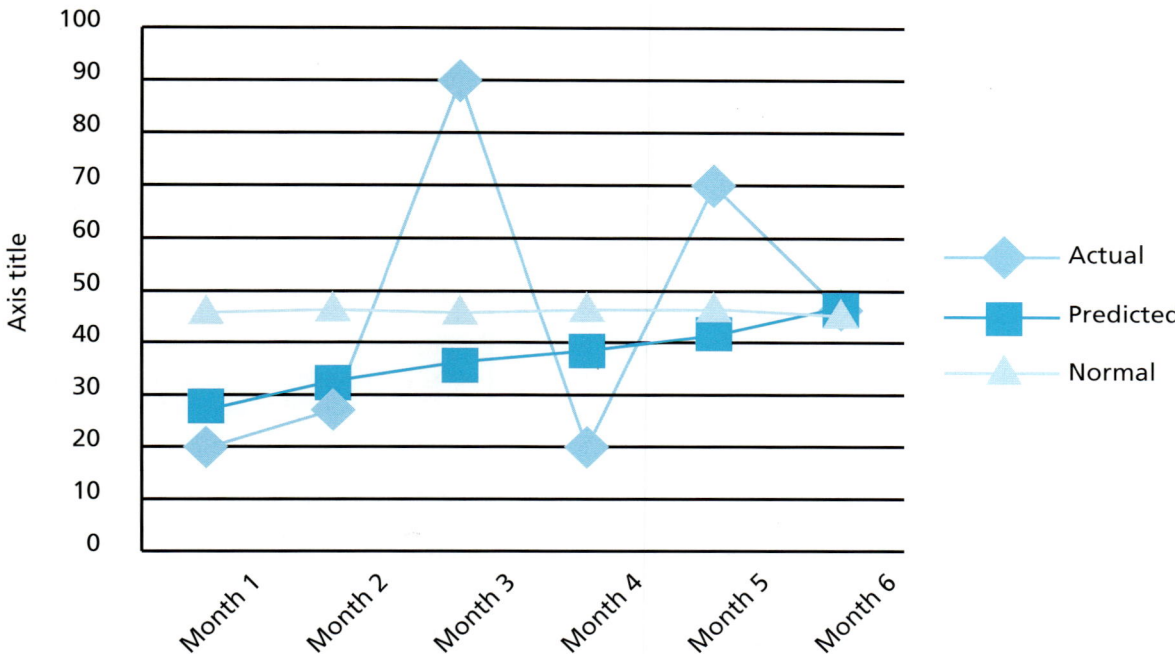

Figure 6.2 Performance tracking

- Accuracy of the performance forecasts
- Resilience of the organization to absorb change.

6.3.2   The benefits test

One of the problems with benefits is that they need to be managed, and to manage anything you need to be able to measure it, so pursuing benefits that cannot be measured is a pointless exercise.

It is very important that benefits are differentiated from desirable things that the organization might want to do.

It is quite often the case that statements are made and included in documentation as benefits, when in fact they are outputs from projects and/or outcomes resulting from changes being implemented.

To technically qualify as a benefit, the description, observable outcomes, attribution and measurement (DOAM) test should be applied. Details of the DOAM test criteria are given in Table 6.8.

If you are unable to attribute or measure the benefit, then it is very likely that you are dealing with an outcome. That is not to say that you can't ever measure or attribute outcomes, but they can be less tangible (e.g. happier staff).

Table 6.8 DOAM test criteria

Description	It should be clear from the description what the positive (or negative for a dis-benefit) effect of the change will be. Normally the benefit would have a positive term associated with it, as with improved, faster, bigger etc., but with a measure to show what is going to be achieved (e.g. reduced service costs by increasing staff productivity by 20%).
Observable outcomes	It should be possible to describe the changes that are required to release the benefit, the outputs from projects, the changes and subsequent outcomes that will need to be achieved.
	So to reduce costs you would need to train staff, improve processes, change working practices and upgrade the production technology.
Attribution	It must be possible to attribute where in the organization improvement will be generated and who is responsible for ensuring it happens. The danger benefits are those that are described vaguely in terms of posts being saved; therefore, the source of the savings should be attributed to business units and cost centres where possible and accounted for in medium-term financial plans.
Measurement	If you can't measure it you can't manage it, and if you cannot manage it then it is unlikely to happen.
	Measures should be able to track the performance change over a period in the lead up, during the transition and after the change has been implemented. It is also helpful to capture a range of measures that show the effect around the change; for example, staff productivity rising is of little help if staff departures increase, you lose customers, or the quality of the products begins to drop.

6.3.3 Building the benefits map

It is tempting to get too preoccupied on what goes into a benefits map. The main purpose of it is to illustrate where and how the benefits will occur.

Mapping all the outputs through to benefits potentially creates a picture that is so complex nobody can understand it. If you are not familiar with the concept, Figure 6.3 gives an example of a map of a simple change from implementing a new production system. The boxes to the left show the capabilities; these are created by the projects.

The lighter grey boxes within the map show outcomes. When a changed state has been achieved in terms of outcomes, the darker grey boxes show the benefits appearing. The box to the right shows the objective being achieved.

By adding a timeline across the bottom to show when the benefits are due to occur you can turn your benefits map into a high-level benefits realization plan. This will give you an indication of when the benefits will appear and is timeline categorization, as it enables you to plan for the benefits release.

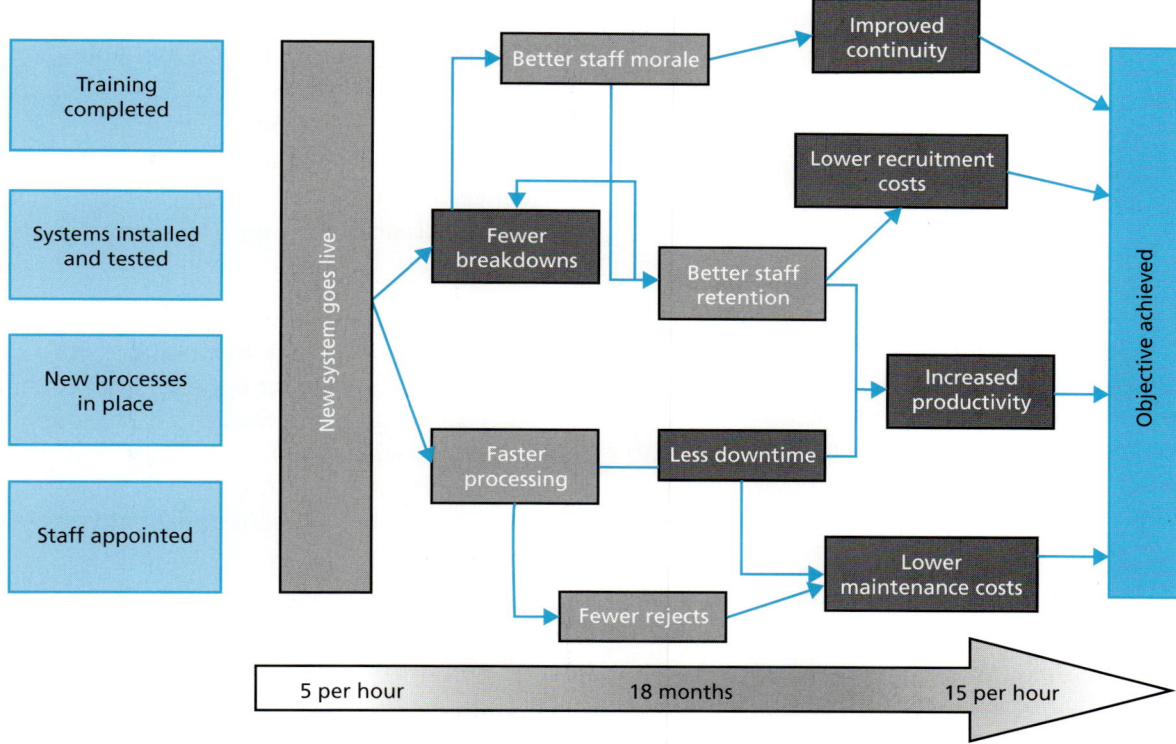

Figure 6.3 Example of flow from capabilities to achievement of objectives

There is a technique called 'investment logic mapping' that is worth investigating if you are looking for more sophistication. This is a more developed concept of benefits mapping and adds values into the capabilities being created and the value of the benefits being released. There are a number of organizations that use this as their basis for the outline business case.

6.3.4 Allocating benefit responsibilities

Within the MSP guide everything to do with benefits tracks back to the BCM, because the BCM is the organization's face within the programme structure and, as such, within the MSP framework, they are personally responsible.

It is important that you make sure that the benefits you are committing to have been actively approved and signed off by the areas where the benefits are going to appear, otherwise the responsibility for failure will track back to you.

Within a business transformation programme this means allocating the benefits to specific cost centres and operational areas. This sounds relatively simple but getting managers to sign up may prove a difficult task. In socio-economic programmes they should be allocated to the key stakeholder organizations.

This is where you may need to call on the SRO and the sponsoring group to help 'encourage' active participation. Leaving the benefits loosely allocated at a high level almost guarantees they will not appear.

For socio-economic programmes or those that are looking to change the behaviour of a market it is quite difficult to encourage change without incentives. It is also difficult to identify who the BCMs for such areas are. In this situation within the programme, someone must assume the role of the BCM as community or sector representative; they should be part of the process of identifying the potential benefits.

6.3.5   What challenges will you face?

There are a number of challenges you will face as the BCM. Hopefully, the information and explanations provided will help set you off in the right direction, but be prepared to deal with one or more of the following:

■ Demands on your time for information to justify the benefit claims

■ Unreasonable expectations of what the potential benefits are

■ Tendency from the SRO to want to get on with it and worry about benefits later

■ Resistance of stakeholders and colleagues to being measured or committing to delivering the benefits

■ Lack of a blueprint or very little information on where the benefits will come from

■ Programme and project teams that are more focused on delivering capabilities than worrying about benefits

■ Failure to focus on risks that will affect benefits rather than project delivery

■ Over-optimism leading to unreasonable estimates and claims

■ Poor-quality information

■ Political pressure to exaggerate benefits to justify the investment

■ Lack of skills and experience to support benefits.

6.3.6   Setting out the detail

You will need to contribute to a number of documents that detail what benefits will be delivered, and where and how this will happen. These were introduced in Figure 3.2 in Chapter 3, and in Appendix A (Table A.2) there is a brief description of each document and what your role should be.

The benefits management strategy sets out the framework within which the programme will operate and deliver benefits.

The benefit profiles are the detailed descriptions of how each benefit will be achieved and measured. You don't want too many of these and it is better to have a small number of well-defined benefits than many diverse and not understood benefits.

The benefits realization plan is the tracking device to ensure your benefits appear and that they are proven and signed off.

6.4   YOUR ROLE IN DEVELOPING THE BENEFITS MANAGEMENT

This is the area that is going to have the majority of focus from you and your team. It is a complex area and it will take commitment to get it right.

You are the pivotal role in benefits management and you need to have high visibility in the programme as the person accountable for the change and the benefits.

6.4.1 Other BCMs

You will need to work closely with other BCMs to establish a 'guiding mind' to ensure that there is a common approach to benefits (defined in the benefits management strategy) that you can all work with. You have to produce the benefit profiles and the detailed analysis that justifies the programme and defines the destination for your part of the organization, including ensuring that there is no double-counting of benefits. The flip side of this is that if the benefits do not justify the programme you are going to need to be courageous and make the position clear.

6.4.2 The SRO

The SRO will ultimately have their reputation on the line so benefits are going to be a very sensitive issue. In some circumstances the SRO will be open to acknowledging the difficulty with benefits as such

an acknowledgement will enable them to ensure that the programme may still need to go ahead, but can't be justified purely on benefits (e.g. in some compliance programmes). In other circumstances the programme may be their personal mission, and a lack of benefits may not be welcomed. Either way you will need to judge the political climate in your organization, but if the benefits don't appear and you say they will, guess who is going to get the blame?

6.4.3 The programme manager

The programme manager is someone you will need to work very closely with as they have to deliver the capabilities from the projects that deliver the benefits. You will need to sign off the projects as the senior manager to ensure they meet your needs. You will also need to ensure that any issues and changes that arise during the project delivery don't undermine the blueprint and remove capabilities you are reliant on.

Table 6.9 shows the key roles in benefits management as given in the MSP guide.

Table 6.9 Key roles in benefits management

Role	Area of focus
Senior responsible owner (SRO)	Reports to the sponsoring group on the delivery of the programme benefits as described in the benefit profiles
	Ensures that the programme and the business areas affected maintain a focus on benefits delivery
	Ensures that the benefits management strategy is created, adjusted, improved and enforced
	Maintains a focus on business performance sustainability during transition
	Chairs benefit reviews involving relevant stakeholders, business managers and possibly internal audits
	Liaises with the sponsoring group on the validation of all benefits claimed by the programme
	Authorizes benefits achievements

Table continues

Table 6.9 *continued*

Role	Area of focus
Programme manager	Develops the benefits management strategy on behalf of the SRO with the BCMs and relevant stakeholders from the affected business areas
	Develops the benefits realization plans in consultation with the BCMs, relevant stakeholders and members of the project teams
	Ensures that the delivery of capability is aligned to maximize the realization of benefits
	Initiates benefit reviews as part of the benefits realization plans or in response to any other triggers
Business change manager(s)	Identifies and quantifies the benefits with the support of relevant stakeholders, the programme manager and members of the project teams
	Delivers particular benefits as profiled: this extends to ensuring that commitments and actions that have been attributed to operational areas are delivered
	Provides information to support the creation and delivery of the benefits realization plan
	Develops and maintains the benefit profiles
	Ensures there is no double-counting of benefits
	Maintains engagement with key individuals responsible for benefits delivery within the operations
	Sets business performance deviation levels and early-warning indicators to support realizing benefits
	Initiates benefit reviews after the programme has closed
Programme office	Monitors the progress of benefits realization against plan
	Gathers information for the benefit reviews
	Produces performance reports as defined by the programme manager
	Maintains benefits information under change control and maintains audit trails of changes

Leadership and stakeholder engagement

7

7 Leadership and stakeholder engagement

'It usually takes more than three weeks to prepare a good impromptu speech.' Mark Twain

The UK National Audit Office has concluded that stakeholder perception is one of the critical factors in whether a programme is a success or failure. There are numerous examples of successful programmes that have delivered their objectives and benefits yet were perceived as a failure, and vice versa: some badly run programmes have failed on all fronts, but were still perceived as a success.

As the business change manager (BCM) and leader of the change in your part of the organization or sector, you are going to be at the forefront of stakeholder engagement.

7.1 BASIC PRINCIPLES

There are plenty of publications and courses on leadership, so this section will concentrate on stakeholders and communications. The root of good practice in this area comes from marketing disciplines, and many of the techniques have evolved from there and been converted for use by programmes. The two key areas to consider are:

- **Stakeholder analysis** The first things you need to know are who the stakeholders are and what they are interested in. It sounds a simple enough requirement, but when you start to look at it more closely it then becomes complex and is often underestimated. You should not just create a contact list that you can send a monthly email to and hope they read it. You and the change team will need to find a way of categorizing them and working out the best way to influence them; high-level groups such as 'staff' are of no use as they are too generic.

Once you know who the stakeholders are and what you think they might be interested in, you will need to know how interested they are, their attitude to your programme (positive or negative), and whether you are going to need things from them or are going to be doing things to them – or both.

- **Communication planning** Once you have identified the stakeholders and understand what they want and don't want, you can target the communications much more effectively and achieve the results you need. Communication is two-way; it is not about you transmitting information but about listening to and understanding the reactions, so you will need to put channels in to deal with this.

> **Example**
>
> After completing the stakeholder session on a BCM course for one of the London councils, one of the senior managers said, 'Crikey, this is a lot of work, but we can either do it up front and maintain some sort of control, or leave it and spend lots of time fire-fighting and responding to challenges when we are in delivery – either way it is going to be a lot of hard work.'

Remember the mnemonic 'SMEF' for good communications:

- **Stakeholder analysis** You need to know what the reaction to your message is going to be and what you want to achieve from it.

- **Message clarity** In the crazy world of endless communications noise you need to be able to get your message heard, so what you are trying to say needs to be clear and concise.
- **Effective channels** You must use the right channels for the audience: there is no point in using Facebook if you want to get to the information security manager! There are many merits in many channels and you need to be clear which ones are going to work for you.
- **Feedback loop** There must be a way for people to provide feedback, whether electronically or face to face. This will help you judge the success of your communications and track the status and commitment to your cause.

7.2 WHAT DOES MSP HAVE TO SAY?

MSP defines a stakeholder as an individual or group that has an interest in the programme, its outcomes or benefits/dis-benefits. There is an inherent link between leadership and stakeholders, which is manifested in the following ways:

- Leaders use the programme vision statement to influence and persuade stakeholders to commit to the beneficial future.
- Business change managers engage their operational stakeholders, leading them through the uncertainty of transition to the new ways of working.
- A focus on benefits recognizes that a 'benefit' is only such when it is perceived to be advantageous by one or more stakeholders. In a community of different interests and attitudes the leader must engage stakeholders so that benefits are identified, clearly communicated and understood, owned and realized, and the threats to realizing those benefits are reduced.

- Some stakeholders will be identified as resources within the delivery of the new capability – some with unique or scarce skills and competencies.

MSP provides advice and guidance on:

- The nature of stakeholder engagement and the need to evaluate and assess their impact and information needs from the programme
- Defining leadership where this has impacts on how stakeholders are engaged and understood including considering internal politics, individual emotions and motivations
- Business change management in the wider context, where a programme may be seen as a part of a larger strategic change initiative or part of a corporate portfolio of change
- Communications in the programme over and above project communications in line with an engagement strategy.

7.2.1 Programme communications plan

The programme communications plan describes what will be communicated, how it will be communicated, when, and by whom, during the programme. It should be designed and implemented as early as possible and then maintained throughout the programme.

Using information from the stakeholder profiles, the activities within the programme communications plan should be designed to:

- Raise awareness among all stakeholders of the benefits and impact of the planned outcomes.
- Gain commitment from stakeholders in the target business area(s) to the changes being introduced – thus ensuring the long-term success of the improvements.
- Keep all stakeholders in the target business area(s) informed of progress before, during and

after implementation or delivery of programme outcomes.

- Promote key messages from the programme.
- Demonstrate a commitment to meeting the requirements of those sponsoring the programme (the sponsoring group).
- Make communications truly two-way (i.e. a dialogue, not a broadcast) by actively encouraging stakeholders to provide feedback and ensuring that they are informed about the use of their feedback to influence the programme. All types of feedback should be expected, and responses to it carefully considered. Feedback may sometimes be negative, impractical or harshly critical.
- Ensure that all those responsible for projects have an understanding of the scope, nature and outcomes of the programme.
- Promote outcomes to maximize the benefits obtained from the new business operations.

Hints and tips

Successful communications are based on four core elements (think 'SMEF'):

- **Stakeholder identification and analysis** Send the right message to the right audience.
- **Message clarity and consistency** Ensure relevance and recognition, and engender trust.
- **Effective system of message delivery** Get the right messages to the right stakeholders in a timely and effective way.
- **Feedback collection system** Assess the effectiveness of the communications process.

7.3 WHAT DOES THIS MEAN TO YOU?

'The degree of one's emotion varies inversely with one's knowledge of the facts – the less you know, the hotter you get.' Bertrand Russell

Stakeholder engagement is up there with benefits and the blueprint as your priority areas. The weaker the stakeholder engagement and communications, the more trouble you are going to experience during the delivery of the programme.

Within the programme management governance, as with most things, the actual responsibilities for structure and management come from the remit of the programme manager. The reason for this, as with the blueprint, is that there could be a number of BCMs but there will only be one programme manager, so by taking this approach there is a single point of responsibility.

The challenge for the BCM is that they need to wear two hats. When they face their organization they are the voice of the programme and as such must promote the concepts sincerely and with passion. When they face the programme they need to wear their organization's hat and equally passionately fight to get the best deal they can.

It is not an easy job and therefore you must be in control of the information that is being released to your organization and must make sure that it is using the right channels, has the right endorsement and is delivered at the right time in the right format. If this doesn't happen you will be the one who has to manage the consequences.

7.3.1 The stakeholder lifecycle and techniques

'Electric communication will never be a substitute for the face of someone who with their soul encourages another person to be brave and true.' Charles Dickens

Table 7.1 MSP high-level stakeholder groups

Group	Description	Examples
Governance	These are the people who will directly or indirectly have a say in the final decision	Senior management
		Shareholders
		Company owners
		Elected representatives
		Regulators
Users	People who will be directly affected by the changes in some way, so will need to survive and buy into the change otherwise they will feel like victims	Staff
		Customers
		Consumers
		Process owners
		Contract owners
Providers	Existing or potential suppliers who will be affected by the changes that the programme will deliver	Existing suppliers
		Product developers
		Potential suppliers
		Market in general
Influencers	People who are on the periphery of the programme and may be little affected by the changes directly, but may be influential so are ignored at your peril	Politicians
		Auditors
		Public opinion
		Programme and project teams
		Quality system people
		Environment and safety

The same common cycle of activities that is found in the themes (see Figure 3.1) applies to stakeholders and communications.

The cycle is continuous and should be embedded in the activities within the programme plan, beginning on Day 1 of the programme. Stakeholder identification is needed to work out who the sponsoring group is and it continues from there.

It is certainly the case that stakeholder engagement comes naturally to some people, and these steps will help to put some structure around what they do naturally. For others it will be opening up a new world of complexity and intrigue.

The following will hopefully provide helpful guidance on each of the four steps.

7.3.1.1 Identify

The first step is to find out who the stakeholders are and to start to build a picture of what it is they are interested in. Before going on a stakeholder hunt, it is worth considering other programmes and projects that are running in your organization. Not only are they potentially stakeholders, but they may already have done some of this work and be targeting similar groups of stakeholders. If you don't do this and communicate separately, the unfortunate recipient may get overloaded with communications: as the BCM, you may experience this yourself from time to time.

MSP categorizes stakeholders into four high-level groups, who may be part of the decision-making process but will have different perspectives on the programme (see Table 7.1).

You can apply the high-level grouping shown in Table 7.1 to your organization and develop it into a specific set of groups that are appropriate to you.

The next challenge is to work out what they might be interested in so that you can segment your audience and be able to target your messages. It isn't very helpful telling staff who are going to be working longer hours how much better off the shareholders will be as a result.

Inexperienced programme teams do the analysis but tend to identify high-level areas of interest (e.g. finance or organizational objectives) when actually most people are interested in what is in it for them and how the programme will affect their role, authority and money.

Table 7.2 An example of a stakeholder map

Area of interest / Stakeholders	Profit margins	Brand impact	Product features	Service quality	Market share	Job security	Timescale
Production staff			✓		✓	✓	✓
Executive board	✓	✓			✓		✓
Call handling staff			✓	✓	✓	✓	
Resellers	✓	✓					✓
End users			✓	✓			✓
Marketing team		✓			✓		✓
Warranty team			✓	✓			✓
Shareholders	✓		✓	✓	✓		✓

There are numerous things within any programme that the stakeholders will be interested in and the list below provides some suggestions:

- Pay and conditions
- Specific benefits
- Process changes
- Technology changes
- Structural changes
- Specific risks
- Market/supply chain changes
- Cost of the programme
- Service levels and quality
- Specific product changes
- Profit levels
- Company perks and benefits.

At the end of the identification step you should be able to produce a stakeholder map, which provides a basic overview of who the audience is and what you think they are interested in. Table 7.2 is a simple example for changes to a product that is being taken to market, with ticks used to show things the different groups of stakeholders may be interested in.

The example in Table 7.2 is purely fictional and no judgement is implied on the various groups. The reality is that you can often find a reason for justifying ticking every box at this stage, which is the reason for a more detailed analysis.

7.3.1.2 Analyse and profile

The source for most of the information needing analysis is you. This is because you should monitor what is going on in the world outside the programme and have contacts in the parts of the organization or sectors you represent so that you can poll opinions and work out how the audience will need to be engaged with and managed.

To undertake the analysis you need to work out the overall impact that the stakeholders are going to have. Figure 7.1 shows this in diagrammatic form.

The first job is to decide on the stakeholder groups that you are going to engage with. Whatever you come up with, there will be overlaps, as there will be individuals or groups that may come under more than one category. For example, in Table 7.2 a reseller could also be a shareholder. You should decide what groupings are optimal for you at the programme stage you are at. It can be helpful to have tiers of groups; for example, a high-level group which is segmented into subgroups for more precise message targeting.

The second job is to confirm that you have got the areas of interest right. As the programme grows so will the number of stakeholder groups and the areas of interest. The engagement needs to be at a level that enables you to target your communications about certain topics most effectively and, again, there may need to be subdivision of the topics to target specific communications effectively.

Figure 7.1 Interest, influence and impact model

The third job is to work out the stakeholders' level of influence on the programme. Influence will come from a mix of two elements:

- **Their level of authority** This authority comes from two potential areas. The first is their position in the hierarchy; ultimately the CEO normally gets their own way. The second is from the level of respect they gain from their knowledge and experience on a particular topic.
- **Their level of interest in the change** If they are highly influential your problem may be that you need to gain their interest or remove it (get them off your back). Similarly, people with little influence but with a lot of interest can make a lot of noise and cause different sorts of problems.

Figure 7.1 shows the relationship between interest, influence and impact. When analysing stakeholders a simple guide to allocating level of impact is the five As (see Figure 7.2):

- **Advocate** Actively supporting you
- **Ally** People who can be relied upon when needed but are less active
- **Ambivalent** Sitting on the fence watching to see which way the wind blows, so passive

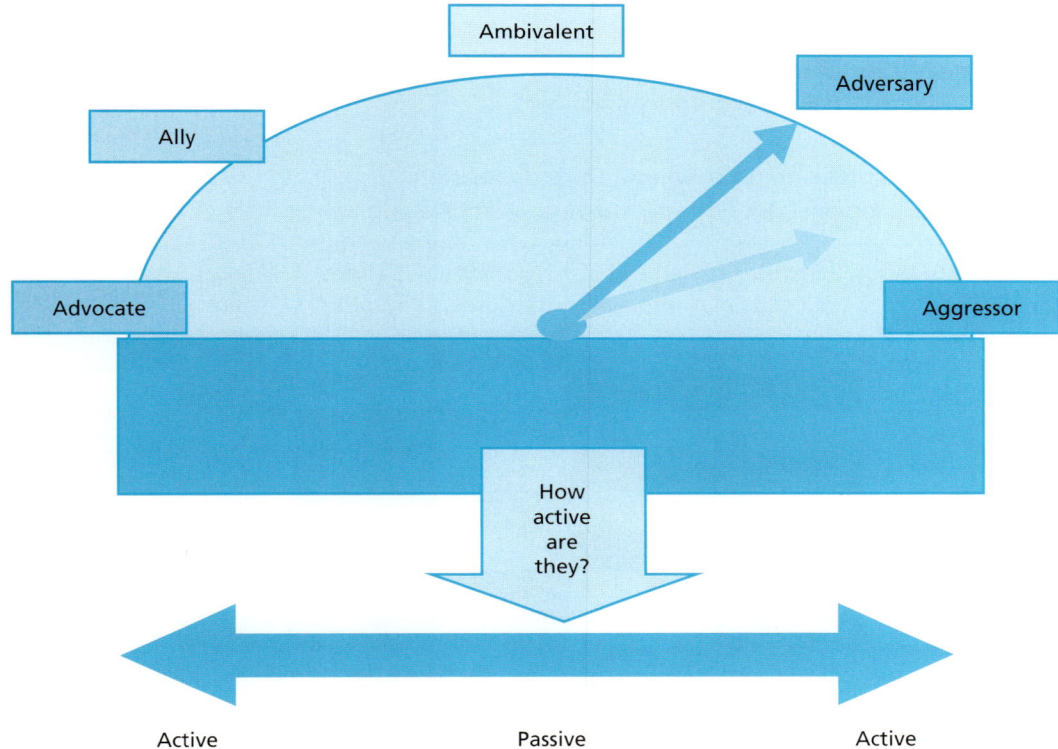

Figure 7.2 The five As of impact

- **Adversary** People who are against you but less active in opposing you
- **Aggressor** Active opponents of the programme.

One thing to be careful of when assessing stakeholders' level of support is that personal prejudices aren't affecting their judgement. Check that they aren't supporting the programme because they happen to like you or trust you, even though they haven't quite understood it yet, and could change position if something changes. A picture should be built up and the conclusions checked out and confirmed with the senior responsible owner (SRO) at least: they will have a good feel for such things.

Once this is done you can enhance your stakeholder map by including a third dimension in the matrix and adding additional information into the cells; shading (dark/medium/light) as shown in Table 7.3

can be used to illustrate the level of support or agreement for a particular area of interest. Remember that it is unlikely that a stakeholder group will support the whole programme; they may have different views on different topics that are building their position of support.

An enhanced stakeholder map as in Table 7.3 gives a good 'at a glance' picture for each of the stakeholder groups but it isn't enough. MSP recommends that a more detailed profile is created, or at least a stakeholder register to store more information, because the summary could be misleading.

For example, there can be different reasons for resistance to the timescales. The board, end users and shareholders want it sooner, whereas the resellers and production staff want it pushed back

Table 7.3 Enhanced stakeholder map showing a third dimension
Shading indicates level of support: dark = strong; medium = ambivalent; light = little or none

Area of interest / Stakeholders	Profit margins	Brand impact	Product features	Service quality	Market share	Job security	Timescale
Production staff			✓		✓	✓	✓
Executive board	✓	✓			✓		✓
Call handling staff			✓	✓	✓	✓	
Resellers	✓	✓					✓
End users			✓	✓			✓
Marketing team		✓			✓		✓
Warranty team			✓	✓			✓
Shareholders	✓		✓	✓	✓		✓

because they don't think they can prepare the market in time. The call handling staff are against it because they don't like change and they are busy enough already. They take that position to every new product!

So there needs to be a deeper understanding of each position, which will enable you to work on transition and migration arrangements to try to meet their concerns – their support or resistance may be based on different reasons.

In benefits management, one of the benefits categories (see section 6.2.1) was stakeholder impact. This related to assessing the level of support for a particular benefit across the stakeholders or tracking whether certain groups of stakeholders were on the receiving end of a lot of benefits, which could cause resistance.

This is illustrated, in the case shown in Table 7.3, by the call handling staff, who have been the subject of a number of efficiency drives and are now working, in their view, excessively hard and are suffering change fatigue. Benefits anticipated for such groups are going to be much harder to achieve.

To assess the stakeholder impact of benefits, you can change the matrix heading in Table 7.3 from 'Area of interest' to 'Benefits'. You can then change the impact to reflect whether they are winners or losers in terms of benefits.

7.3.1.3 Measure and plan

Now that you have done the analysis you will have the baseline against which the success of the communications can be measured. Maintenance of the stakeholder profiles should be an ongoing activity and their status should be reviewed by the programme board as a standing agenda item.

For each group you should decide what the communications plan needs to achieve, so you will need to work out:

- What level of support you will need from them
- How active they will need to be

Table 7.4 Smythe and McKinsey model

Approach	Summary	Outcome
Telling	Telling the many what has been decided by the few (instructional with little sell)	Hooligans or spectators
Selling	Selling to the many what has been decided by the few (tell with a sell and entertainment)	Compliant collaborators
Involving	Driving accountability down by including and engaging people as individuals (giving people the time, space and process to apply the change/decision to their own work, regardless of the degree of delegation)	Willing collaborators
Co-creation	Judging who will add value if included in front-end decision forming and change/strategy development. This is not to be confused with a laissez-faire culture, which is poor at closure and ill-disciplined; co-creation takes robust governance and skill	Personally committed reformers

- Where they are on the level of engagement at the moment
- What channels are going to work best for them
- Who will be most effective in delivering the message
- When will be the best time to engage them.

Table 7.4 is a model from work by John Smythe (2008) that helps us to understand how different approaches will cause different reactions.

Example

During a restructuring programme of three IT departments across England, each group reacted to the announcements very differently. One decided they couldn't do much about it, so there was no point in worrying but were active in contributing ideas, another had a young workforce who weren't too worried about job security and were ambivalent and didn't participate too much, and the third were hostile throughout.

When the announcement was finally made that there would be one centre, reductions would be by natural wastage and there were promotion opportunities, the hostile group actually called the ICT director a liar. In the days that followed the IT manager for that area was removed and given a different role. Within weeks the whole mood in the group changed and the hostile group accepted the situation and got on with it.

The lesson learned was that the local manager had reflected their own personal anxiety into the team, which was generating the hostility.

7.3.1.4 Deliver and review

'We cling to our own point of view, as though everything depended on it. Yet our opinions have no permanence; like autumn and winter, they gradually pass away.' Chuang Tzu

There is always a temptation to run headlong into launches and announcements without fully understanding the audience: equally, delaying communications just raises suspicions that whatever the change is that is coming, it is going to be bad.

It is important when delivering information to take people on a 'journey' and feed them the information they need to know at the appropriate time. This journey can also be seen as a cycle (see Figure 7.3), which has its origins in sales and marketing.

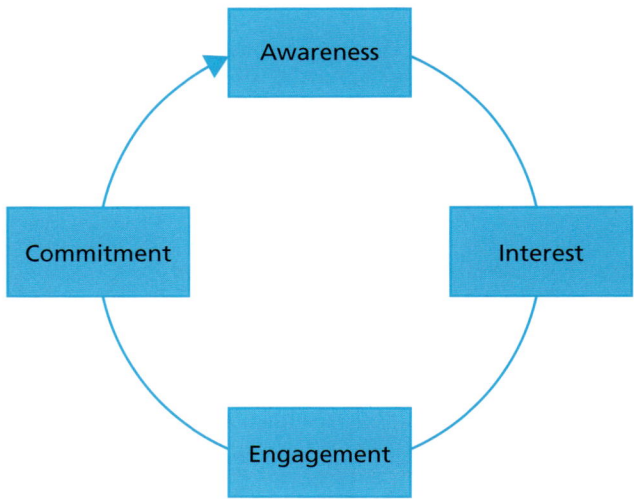

Figure 7.3 Information delivery cycle

As an example of such a cycle, a car manufacturer would use general TV advertising to generate awareness of the brand and the features. Your interest would be stimulated either by a change of your circumstances (your car breaks down) or some local promotion that triggers you to act and engage with them by visiting the sales showroom. After that the sales people take over and take you through to commitment (and signing on the dotted line) by matching their product to your needs.

You can apply this approach to your communications delivery: if an individual is unaware or only vaguely aware of a change, there is no point in giving them a 20-page document to read or even trying to get a meeting in their diary.

You and your team should take them on a journey, to raise their awareness and convince them there is something in it for them. Hopefully, this will generate interest and you will have earned the right to engage them. If you haven't followed the journey and go straight in and are refused a meeting, it doesn't mean they are against the programme; it just means you haven't communicated well with them. If this happens, there is a danger that you characterize them as aggressors when they aren't.

Once you have engaged them you can explain the issues and the approach. It may well be that they are still not in favour, but they will understand the situation and, even if you don't gain an advocate, you may well have avoided having an aggressor. They will also appreciate being consulted.

Tracking and review should be conducted at regular intervals. The effectiveness of the communications can be tracked by using the three-dimensional stakeholder map to see how the mood is changing and whether communications have been successful.

Table 7.5 Revised three-dimensional stakeholder map
Shading indicates level of support: dark = strong; medium = ambivalent; light = little or none

Area of interest / Stakeholders	Profit margins	Brand impact	Product features	Service quality	Market share	Job security	Timescale
Production staff			✓		✓	✓	✓
Executive board	✓	✓			✓		✓
Call handling staff			✓	✓	✓	✓	
Resellers	✓	✓					✓
End users			✓	✓			✓
Marketing team		✓			✓		✓
Warranty team			✓	✓			✓
Shareholders	✓		✓	✓	✓		✓

Table 7.5 is based on Table 7.3 but shows the position after a new product launch communication. As you can see, everyone has been convinced that the timing is right and even the call handling staff have moved to 'ambivalent'. The end users still want more features but they will have to wait for the next release!

7.4 YOUR ROLE IN LEADERSHIP AND STAKEHOLDER ENGAGEMENT

This theme is critical to you as a BCM: if communications are handled well then your life will be much easier, but if they are handled badly then your job will become exponentially more difficult.

7.4.1 Other BCMs

With the other BCMs you will need to work as a team on this and you may choose to have a dedicated communications person in the business change team to work on behalf of you all. It is not a trivial job to do the stakeholder analysis and communications tracking. You definitely do not want to find yourself in a position where there are conflicting messages coming out of the programme and the best place to start is to ensure that the BCMs are all agreed when it comes to communications and control of the communications release process.

7.4.2 The SRO

The SRO is likely to be more influential and have better contacts with the executive and powerful interests, so you will need to work closely with them. They will also be extremely concerned about maintaining stakeholder engagement and support. They will not want the big players drifting away from the table as their reputation is at stake.

7.4.3 The programme manager

With the programme manager you will need to ensure that the right controls are in place and that there is a stakeholder engagement strategy that you have signed up to and the SRO has signed off. The danger is that projects communicate separately from the programme; apart from showing a lack of control it is also dangerous because the project perspective on a scenario or progress may be different from that of the programme and your organization. A particular project could be going very well and be broadcasting positive messages during a period of high stakeholder resistance, or the opposite could be true: the project could be sending out negative messages when there is a very positive feel around the programme. So you need to agree how the management controls work and make sure you are in the approval chain.

Table 7.6 is a summary of roles and areas of focus from MSP.

Table 7.6 Key roles in leadership and stakeholder engagement

Role	Area of focus
Senior responsible owner (SRO)	Engaging key stakeholders early and at appropriate milestones throughout the programme
	Leading the engagement with high-impact stakeholders and anticipating stakeholder issues that may arise
	Briefing the sponsoring group and gathering strategic guidance on changing business drivers
	Showing visible leadership at key communications events and ensuring the visible and demonstrable commitment of the sponsoring group
	Ensuring the creation, implementation and maintenance of the overall stakeholder engagement strategy
Programme manager	Developing and implementing the stakeholder engagement strategy
	Day-to-day implementation of the whole stakeholder engagement process
	Developing and maintaining the stakeholder profiles
	Controlling and aligning project communications activities
	Ensuring effective communications with the project teams
	Developing, implementing and updating the programme communications plan
Business change manager(s)	Engaging and leading those operating new working practices through the transition, generating confidence and buy-in from those involved. Active stakeholder engagement is a major part of discharging this role
	Supporting the SRO and taking specific responsibility for stakeholder engagement in their part of the organization
	Support to the programme manager in the development of the stakeholder engagement strategy and programme communications plan
	Alerting the programme manager to the net winners and losers (if any) in their area of change
	Providing information and business intelligence for the stakeholder profiles
	Briefing and liaising with the business change team
	Communicating with affected stakeholders to identify new benefits and improved ways of realizing benefits
	Delivering key communications messages to their business operations
Programme office	Maintaining information relating to the stakeholders
	Maintaining an audit trail of communication activity
	Collating feedback and ensuring that it is logged and processed
	Facilitating activities specified in the programme communications plan

Risk and issue management

8

8 Risk and issue management

'What we anticipate seldom occurs, what we least expect generally happens.'
Benjamin Disraeli

The business change managers (BCMs) are responsible for managing some of the biggest risks in a change programme, namely that the programme will cause a loss in business performance stability during the change or will fail to deliver the benefits on which the investment was justified. Both of these risks have your name against them so this is a topic you should be very focused on even if (as in the example given) your first reaction is that talking about what can go wrong is rather dull.

Example

A BCM on a programme board that was discussing risks and issue management said 'Ugh, here we go entering techie world.' This was a very interesting comment, as she was a highly competent senior human resources manager who was totally engaged in the process but didn't feel risks applied to her. The programme manager was left wondering what was going wrong as they were doing what it said in the book. Risk is often a discussion about all the things that could go wrong and can be depressing – so the challenge is how to make it interesting. Part of the art of a good programme manager is to stop risk management being dull and make it real for people: it is important that the BCMs see it as something that is real and engage with the process to make it effective.

8.1 BASIC PRINCIPLES

In summary, risks are things that might happen, while issues are things that have happened. Both require management. Supporting them are the concepts of change control and configuration management, which is often linked to issue management.

Risk management is the management of uncertainty. It can be positive or negative. Most programmes happily occupy themselves with the negative effects but by including the opportunities as well it helps to keep the discussion more positive. In reality successful programmes often do have a bit of luck and with good risk management getting lucky can become a habit. Gary Player, the golfer, said: 'The more I practise, the luckier I get.'

Risk is real and it has been said that one of the worst things that happened to risk management was the risk register. It gives the impression of risks being linear when, in fact, risks are relational and interconnected. When things go wrong it is the interconnectivity of the risks that causes the major problems; it is rarely a single risk.

This is why it is much better to focus on the threat or the root cause. If you think about the London 2012 Olympics, there was a major threat of a terrorist attack. However, there were many ways it could have occurred and there were many potential effects; breaking down a risk into its component parts can help everyone understand the risk and make it more tangible to manage.

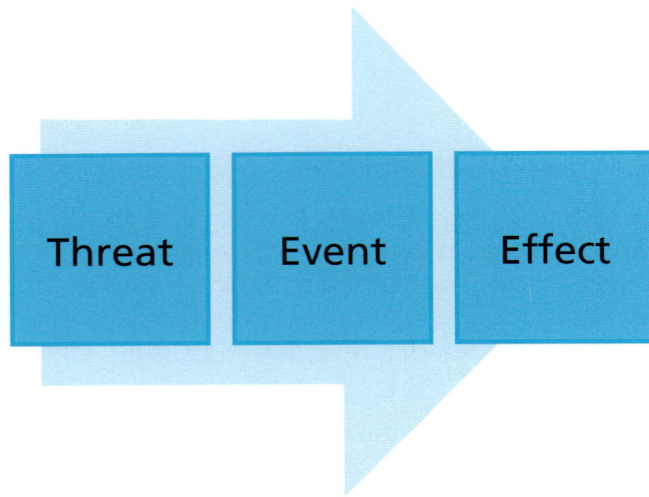

Figure 8.1 Threat, event and effect flow

You will probably find that you have a mix of threats, events and effects on your risk register. By focusing on the threats, you can also very quickly reduce the risk register from an endless list of the things that might go wrong to a more focused document where you manage the threats or events rather than worrying about the effects (see Figure 8.1).

Issue management is the management of problems that have arisen as a result of unplanned events that have happened, changes that are being requested, or unexpected or anticipated obstacles. It is an activity that fills a lot of time for programme teams. If the team is not great at risk management, they end up with a lot of issues and there is a danger that the list gets bigger and bigger, so you must ensure there is a way of resolving the issues and also categorizing them in terms of priority and impact.

Change control is the key to the effective delivery of the blueprint. It must happen at the programme level but there are dangers at the project level.

Individual projects may be working within their permitted tolerances but the aggregating effect of a dozen projects all being 10% over on their budgets or time can have a massive effect on the ability to deliver change and release benefits. Therefore the management of project scope should be based on an impact assessment that includes the programme blueprint.

As the BCM, you will have to watch out for local changes in the way the organization or sector operates and the impact on the blueprint (and potential loss of benefits) that can result. It is important to ensure that all requests for changes to projects and programmes are managed through the issue register and established process to ensure that they are properly tracked.

Configuration management is basically version and relationship control of assets. Whether the asset is a manufacturing unit, a bill for parliament, IT software or a programme document, it is important that the status is tracked, the changes are authorized, and that it has some sort of version control. This is covered by the information management strategy and is very much in the remit of the programme manager and the programme office.

8.2 WHAT DOES MSP HAVE TO SAY?

MSP defines a risk as an uncertain event or set of events which, should it occur, will have an effect on the achievement of objectives. This effect need not necessarily be detrimental. A risk can be either a 'threat' (i.e. an uncertain event that could have a negative impact on objectives or benefits) or an 'opportunity' (i.e. an uncertain event that could have a favourable impact on objectives or benefits).

The task of programme risk management is to ensure that the programme makes cost-effective use of a risk management process that includes a series of well-defined steps. The aim is to support better decision-making through a good understanding of risks and their likely impact.

Risks and issues can emerge from a variety of sources – for example:

- Benefits management, transition activities, costs, scope and timescales
- Dependencies, constraints, assumptions, quality of operations, resources and programme deliverables
- Anything that cannot be resolved within a project, or issues common to more than one project
- Stakeholders, organization and programme staff, and third parties
- Degradation of operational performance beyond acceptable levels
- Ambiguity or lack of knowledge about the 'as-is' state, the interim state and the desired end state
- Other projects and programmes under way within the organization.

There are four perspectives to risk management, which reflect the types of risk that a programme will be required to manage (see Table 8.1).

Table 8.1 Risk management perspectives

Strategic	Changes at the strategic level can affect the programme, its interdependencies with other initiatives and ultimately its outcomes and benefits realization.
Programme	Programmes focus on delivering benefits to the organization and often affect a wide variety of stakeholders both internally and externally, positively and negatively. Risk management for a programme must be designed to work across organizational boundaries in order to accommodate these differing interests and ensure that stakeholders are engaged appropriately.
Project	The project outputs within a programme are the vehicles for delivering the programme outcomes and benefits; therefore, much of the focus of risk and issue management within a programme is from the project perspective. The programme should set the risk and issue management standards for the project and then give staff the authority to manage their risks and issues within these parameters.
	To manage the risks to projects well, the programme needs to ensure that each project brief outlines the risks from the perspective of the programme and then request the project to provide regular feedback to the programme's risk management activities.
Operational	As projects deliver their outputs, the transition to new ways of working and new systems can lead to further sources of risk. For example, during a handover process, risks and issues could arise from the need to maintain operational stability as well as the integrity of the systems, infrastructure and support services. Transition must therefore be properly planned, managed and resourced.

8.2.1   Principles of risk management

The key principles for risk management at programme level are that it:

- Aligns with objectives
- Fits the context
- Engages stakeholders
- Provides clear guidance
- Informs decision-making
- Facilitates continual improvement
- Creates a supportive culture
- Achieves measurable value.

8.2.2   Managing risks in a programme

Before the risk management cycle can operate, the specific arrangements for managing risk should specify:

- Risk appetite
- Tolerance thresholds
- Assumptions
- Early-warning indicators
- Risk register content
- Threat and opportunity
- Evaluating risks
- Risk aggregation
- Proximity
- Progress reporting.

There are a number of potential responses to any risk, namely:

- Avoid a threat or exploit an opportunity
- Reduce a threat or enhance an opportunity
- Transfer the risk
- Share the risk
- Accept the risk
- Prepare contingency plans.

8.2.3   Managing issues in a programme

Issues can occur at any point from the launch of the programme at the beginning of Identifying a Programme to when the programme closes. Some issues may be unresolved at the end of the programme and responsibility for these may need to be transferred to operational management.

The management action required may be to fix a problem or to change the boundary of the programme. An issue generally emerges from one of a number of sources, for example:

- Constraints identified at the outset of the programme
- Within the programme itself
- In operational areas to be changed by the programme, where these have a consequential impact on the programme
- Escalated from a programme's constituent projects
- Generated by stakeholders
- Other sources external to the programme (e.g. changes to corporate strategy or conflicts with other concurrent change initiatives).

Issues that occur in a project may need to be escalated if they fall outside the project's tolerance levels set by the programme. Issue management in a programme needs to cover all of these circumstances.

A common cause of overload in a programme is when it tries to manage the project issues directly and does not effectively manage escalation and delegation. However, the programme manager does need to be satisfied that the project teams are managing issues to a satisfactory standard and that the aggregated impact on the programme from all issues in all its projects is understood and acceptable.

Issues can typically be classified into one of the following three types:

- A previously identified risk that has now materialized and requires appropriate issue management action
- A request for change to some aspect of the programme, an operation or a project
- A problem affecting all or part of the programme in some way.

8.2.4 Change control

Programmes are inherently about delivering change but they do not exist in isolation as changes are happening to the environment they are delivering to all the time. This can result in changing business requirements, reactions to unplanned events or failures, and loss of stakeholder confidence, all of which can affect the ability of the programme to deliver its objectives. There is a particular risk that small changes across a number of projects may conflict and, because of their apparent insignificance, they may pass through unnoticed.

The basic steps of change control are:

- Capture the change and define why it is needed
- Allocate a priority so that the urgency is understood
- Assess the impact across the programme
- Analyse the options and test the potential solutions
- Authorize the resolution that is agreed (which could include no action)
- Implement the change and monitor the effects of the change for deviations from what is anticipated
- Review the effectiveness and update associated documentation.

All changes should undergo an assessment that considers their impact on at least the following:

- Programme plan
- Blueprint
- Benefits
- Projects dossier.

8.2.5 Configuration management

The purpose of configuration management in a programme is to control the development of, and changes to, items that are important to the programme. These items include programme management documentation as well as the assets, products and services created by the programme. Configuration management covers the programme's dependencies on items outside its control as well as those within the programme.

There are five basic processes involved in programme-level configuration management:

- Planning
- Identifying
- Controlling
- Status accounting
- Verifying.

8.3 WHAT DOES THIS MEAN TO YOU?

'The first principle is that you must not fool yourself, and you are the easiest person to fool.'
Richard P. Feynman

Risks are what will cause the programme to go wrong and if you aren't in control of them your job will be a nightmare.

It is very tempting to think risks and issues are the domain of the programme manager and the project teams and, day to day, this tends to be the case. In reality the effects of these risks are going to lie with you as most of them will affect your ability to deliver the changes and the benefits.

The earlier you engage with the risk process the sooner your authority will be felt within the programme. You are not a bystander: you are the one with the toughest job and that needs to be understood.

The relationship between corporate risk and programme risk needs to be understood by you and the senior responsible owner (SRO). In some circumstances the programme will be creating an organizational risk, for example performance stability during change. It can also be dealing with a corporate risk, for example legislative compliance. It may also be having a number of effects on other corporate risks and their status.

Having a specific risk management strategy that sets these things out is very important. There may be programme risks that have no bearing or impact on corporate risks, which is why having clear definitions, boundaries and escalation techniques to and from corporate risk is important.

8.3.1   What do you need to do?

There are some key areas that you should keep an eye on which will help:

■ Corporate risk processes which pick up operational risks have a tendency to operate in a parallel universe to the programme and project risks. Everyone nods sagely and says this isn't a problem but the fact is that it is a problem. You are the bridgehead between operations and the programme so you need to keep an eye on both universes to ensure they are aligned and that no gaps are developing.

■ The business change team are important within this. Just as the project teams will be maintaining their project risk register, you should consider having a risk register of your own. You can then manage the medium- and low-level risks locally and only use the programme board as a point of escalation to keep the risks realistic at that level.

■ The business change team are also going to be working with the projects and they are your intelligence network. By having internal discussions you may find you know about aggregating issues and risks across the projects that the project teams or the programme manager haven't spotted.

8.3.2   Risk and issue management cycles and you

'All courses of action are risky, so prudence is not in avoiding danger (it's impossible), but calculating risk and acting decisively. Make mistakes of ambition and not mistakes of sloth. Develop the strength to do bold things, not the strength to suffer.' Niccolò Machiavelli

Risk and issue management has the same cycle as you have seen in the other themes (see Figure 3.1). Here are some ideas to help you through because, whether you like it or not, risk and issue management is very important to you and there are things to watch out for.

8.3.2.1 Identify

The programme may have come into existence to manage a potential risk to a market or legal position. In that situation much of the risk will be about not meeting this challenge and the consequences.

MSP identifies the four types of risk and the BCM should focus on strategic and operational, but particularly the latter.

This doesn't mean you can ignore project and programme risk and there is a particular aspect called 'aggregation', which is the domino or cocktail effect of risks affecting each other (see section 8.3.2.2 below). Anything that happens in the project world will threaten your benefits and blueprint.

Table 8.2 provides a checklist of threats to look for during the Identify step of the cycle.

8.3.2.2 Analyse and profile

There tends to be a focus on completing lines of risk in a register but there is value in profiling the risk (in the same way that you would profile a benefit or a stakeholder) to understand the root cause of the threat and how it would manifest itself.

In the example in Figure 8.2, the threat is the same, but there are a number of ways it could be caused

Table 8.2 Threats to look for during the Identify step

Threat	Description
Staff resistance	This can be caused by many things, such as fear of the unknown, poor communications or existing antagonistic relations that your programme will encounter.
Poor information about current processes	When you try to change things you don't fully understand, there is a risk that you will miss something, in particular where local custom and practice have evolved to cover gaps in the service or process. Removing key individuals will suddenly cause gaps to appear and unexpected service failures to start happening.
Management resistance	The top layer of the organization may be committed to the changes but the middle management layers are like the organizational cement and can provide the most structured, intangible resistance. There may also be issues with the senior managers and these need to be dealt with as well.
Poor information related to performance	The benefits are based on improvements in performance of some sort: if the information available is of dubious quality, the risk of non-achievement of benefits will be higher as the basis for calculation will be flawed.
Lack of clarity about the future state	If the programme doesn't have a blueprint with a clear target operating model, then basically the programme doesn't know where it is going and it will end up being led by the projects.
Maintaining acceptable performance	If the operational performance is not monitored and controlled, then deteriorations can happen – not just during transition but also in the pre-transition phase as the focus is lost or morale drops.

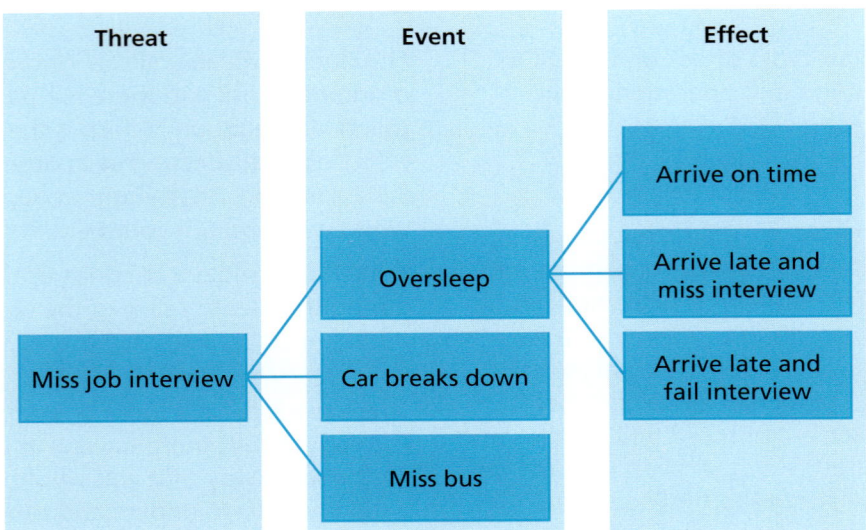

Figure 8.2 Threat, event and effect profile

and the effects could be the same or different for each of the events. It is a straightforward illustration, but if you profile risks and build simple maps to show the effects, similar to benefits maps, you will understand the risk much better and the effect it could have on your programme.

The result of this profiling work may well make it clear that the programme faces far more risk than was anticipated and may cause the sponsoring group to have a rethink. The earlier this happens the better, as the SRO must accept the level of risk they are taking.

When undertaking profiling, consider two areas:

■ **Domino or cascade effect** If the threat materializes from an event, what other threats or opportunities could be triggered as well? This could cause a domino effect to occur that would have a bigger effect than the individual risks in isolation.

■ **Cocktail effect** If a number of the threats happen simultaneously but are largely unconnected, what would the total effect be? The mitigation plans may be able to cope with one risk materializing but what are the dependencies between plans (e.g. key resources)?

For you to be effective, it is critical to ensure you have a good understanding of the cause and effect between project risks and the impact on operations, and the impact of a major operational risk hitting the programme or a project.

Although it sounds obvious, be clear if you are managing a risk or an issue. The techniques are different. While a lot of time can be spent trying to mitigate an event that is certain to happen (the issue), it is actually the effects of the event that are uncertain. It is these that present the risk and must be managed.

Example

If your programme could be affected by an upcoming election, the election is an issue as it is going to happen and you will have to deal with the consequences. The risk is a change of political direction, which could have legislative impact on your programme.

8.3.2.3 Measure and plan

In terms of measurement, you need good information on your baseline performance so that you can track any deviation in performance that could be an early-warning indicator of an emerging risk. Your focus is principally on operational risk so having the ability to monitor trends is essential.

Another important area to measure is stakeholder support. If there is increased resistance then the situation will become less stable and more difficult to manage.

Each of the risks should have contingency plans in place to deal with the 'what if' scenarios should situations materialize.

The programme manager will probably produce a probability impact grid such as the one in Table 8.3 to help plan the intensity of the management of individual risks. The ones with high probability and high impact are going to receive a lot more focus than those that are perceived to be under control.

In Table 8.3, where a risk is in the dark zone the reviews and management would be more intense, possibly weekly; where the risk is in the medium zone it could be a monthly review; and where a risk is in the light zone then it could be quarterly.

8.3.2.4 Deliver and review

The effectiveness of the delivery will be reflected in the size of the issue register: if it is large then it will mean that the risks are not being well managed, but that is often the reality of the situation. It is particularly a problem with emergent programmes because many of the projects are already rolling and difficult to bring under control, so issues tend to dominate.

Your focus should be on operational risks and managing them. Some of the common threats are also certain to arise so you could argue they are issues before you start.

You should also keep a close eye on project risks and issues and how they may trigger problems for you. Your business change team must play an important role in this; embed them within the project boards or project teams so that you know what is going on.

Table 8.3 Example of a probability impact grid
Shading indicates priority of risk: dark = high; medium = average; light = low

	Very low impact	Low impact	Medium impact	High impact	Very high impact
Highly likely					
Likely					
Medium					
Unlikely					
Highly unlikely					

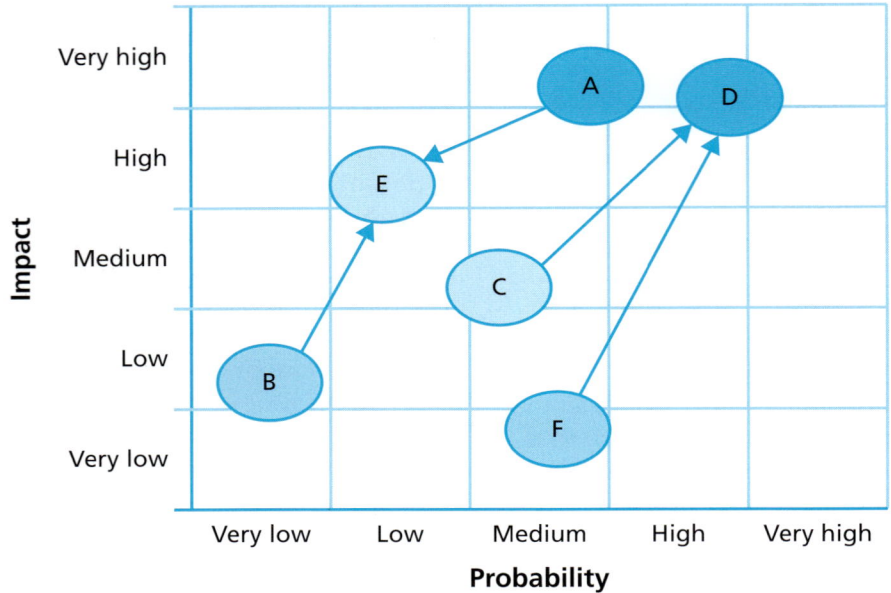

Figure 8.3 Tracking aggregated risks

Table 8.4 Key roles in risk and issue management

Role	Area of focus
Senior responsible owner (SRO)	Authorizes the risk management strategy and issue management strategy and its adjustment, improvement and enforcement
	Intervenes to control risks and issues that affect the alignment of the programme with organizational objectives
	Initiates assurance reviews of risk and issue management effectiveness
	Has ownership of strategic risks and issues, and ensures mitigation actions are dealt with at the appropriate senior level
Programme manager	Develops and implements the strategies for handling risks and issues
	Designs and manages the risk and issue management cycle
	Manages the aggregated level of risks and issues
	Assures programme adherence to the risk management principles
	Allocates risks and issues as appropriate

Table continues

Role	Area of focus
Programme manager *continued*	Ensures that change control is undertaken by individuals with the correct authority
	Ensures that the impact of individual and aggregated risks is understood by the relevant stakeholders
	Defines clear rules for escalation, cascade and thresholds
	Has ownership of programme-level risks and issues
	Deploys a consistent language for risk management across the programme and its projects
	Communicates progress on the resolution of issues in a clear and timely fashion across the programme
	Escalates items that cross programme boundaries to the SRO for resolution where necessary
	Design and implementation of the configuration management system
Business change manager(s)	Manages and coordinates the resolution of risks relating to operational performance and benefits achievement
	Ensures that the risk management cycle includes operational risks
	Manages risks that impact on business performance and transition
	Identifies operational issues and ensures that they are managed by the programme
	Identifies opportunities from the business operations and raises them for inclusion in the programme
	Contributes to impact assessments and change control
	Monitors and reports on business performance issues that may require the attention of the programme during transition
Programme office	Manages and coordinates the information and support systems to enable efficient handling of the programme's risks and issues
	Maintains the programme risk register
	Maintains the programme issue register
	Establishes, facilitates and maintains the risk management cycle
	Establishes, facilitates and maintains the issue management cycle
	Provides support and advice on the risks and issues to projects
	Coordinates risk and issue management interfaces with projects
	Maintains the configuration management system
	Facilitates the change control steps

As mentioned before, the key concern for the BCM should be about aggregating the level of risk and understanding how the various risks and issues are moving and may be playing off against each other.

Quite often the level of danger is hidden within pages and pages of a risk register. It may be useful to draw the potential relationship between risks, as illustrated in Figure 8.3. This captures your risks on a 'radar' so that you can see how they are interrelated and if they are moving around.

In the simple example shown in Figure 8.3, risk A could trigger risk E and so could risk B. If E and B are becoming more likely, the overall level of risk will be rising, as will the potential impact.

In real life, a chart such as that shown in Figure 8.3 often ends up needing an A3 sheet to show all the risks, but it is much more effective in getting the attention of people than wading through pages of paper at each project board. If nothing else, produce something like this for the risks that affect you and use it to communicate with your teams.

8.4 YOUR ROLE IN RISK AND ISSUE MANAGEMENT

The majority of responsibility for risk and issue management sits with the programme manager but you have an important role to play as part of the programme board.

8.4.1 Other BCMs

As always, you need to build a relationship and work as a team with the other BCMs. It is likely that the risks will be similar for all of you, but the local effects will be different. The aggregating effect of risks across the organization will be one of the key areas for you all to work on.

8.4.2 The SRO

For the SRO, risks are the things that are going to cost them their job if they miss something important. It isn't unknown for SROs to want to ignore the reality of the situation and take the position 'just sort it out'. However, this creates a culture of risk suppression that is particularly dangerous. Their focus will be on the strategic risks, so bear that in mind. In your relationship with the SRO, you will need to find a way to engage with them constructively and provide honest and open advice. Try not to be the bearer of problems and try to bring forward the problem together with some potential solutions to help them with the decision.

8.4.3 The programme manager

You will be depending on the programme manager for structure. The programme manager is in charge of the strategies for risk, issue and information management, all of which affect you, so you will need to ensure you have contributed to their development. The processes and tools that are used will be the responsibility of the programme manager, so you need to work closely with that person to ensure that the processes and tools work for you and are pragmatic. The programme manager will also be keeping track of the projects and programme risks. The big areas you must know about are anything that threatens the blueprint or the benefits: decisions on these will come down to you.

Table 8.4 shows the key roles in risk and issue management and is taken from MSP. It sets out the specific areas of focus that MSP has defined for you and the other roles.

Planning and control 9

9 Planning and control

'Nothing defines humans better than their willingness to do irrational things in the pursuit of phenomenally unlikely payoffs.' Scott Adams

This theme isn't called planning and control by accident. It is in two parts: the first covers developing the programme plan and the second covers controlling the programme delivery based on the plan.

From your point of view as the business change manager (BCM) a lot of the detail concerning planning revolves around capability building and project delivery, because this is where the money is going to be spent, and everyone worries about money.

Part of the reason why benefits tend to be forgotten about is because all the focus goes on building things rather than what happens once they are built and how the benefits will be released.

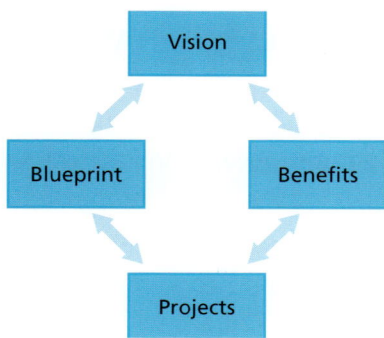

Figure 9.1 The relationship between vision, blueprint, benefits and projects

Planning brings together the vision, the blueprint and benefits and helps to define the projects needed to enable the requirements from them to be met (see Figure 9.1). So, if you have projects and no benefits or blueprint, something is going to go wrong.

9.1 BASIC PRINCIPLES

'Plans are nothing; planning is everything.' Dwight D. Eisenhower

This section provides a brief summary of the key concepts within the planning and control theme.

The **programme plan** is often an amalgam of other documents. Within MSP there are a number of plans that need to be developed and managed; for example, the quality and assurance plan, resource management plan, programme communications plan and benefits realization plan. So the programme plan could be one document with many parts or comprise a number of separate documents.

What the programme plan isn't is a massive Microsoft® Project or Gantt chart which shows what all the projects are doing in some sort of master plan. That is the programme schedule, and if that is what you are seeing as the programme plan, then it is quite probably already out of control.

The detailed plans covering transition and benefits realization will often sit in operations, with the programme plan drawing together the various aspects into a format that can be understood by the programme board. Some ingenuity in how the plan is presented may well be required.

Projects dossier is the MSP term used for the collection of projects that the programme will deliver to create the capability. It is rather an odd phrase and some organizations use the term project portfolio instead, but this can be confused with portfolio management. Increasingly, the term project register is being used for the document that contains the key project information. It should contain enough information to initiate a project and the contents will evolve as the programme progresses; more or fewer projects may be required depending on how things pan out.

Tranches are a very important and often missing concept and underpin control. Programmes often become unwieldy due to their size and tranches help to manage that. They are used to group projects and focus efforts on achieving a 'step change' in capability; this avoids lots of expenditure on many fronts with no clarity about how it all comes together. Tranches are time and achievement bound. They are closely linked to the blueprint intermediate states; at the end of a tranche an intermediate state will have been delivered. So, the intermediate state in 2015 shown in Figure 5.6 would be the end of a tranche.

Tranches provide an opportunity to stand back, take stock and decide whether the blueprint end state is still where you want to go, whether the benefits are validated, genuine and achievable, and whether you can still afford to get there. It is also an opportunity either to gracefully exit the programme if it is no longer required or to re-energize it if it has lost some momentum.

Workstreams are a way of grouping projects by type so that resources can be concentrated and dedicated to certain activities; for example, you could have a property workstream or an ICT workstream. These are not bound by time and a workstream could run through the life of the programme. You could have a workstream dedicated to your organization, for example.

A **dependency network** is a technique that helps to illustrate how the various elements of the programme fit together, rather like a jigsaw puzzle. It is a key element of control as it shows how the inputs and outputs from the various projects fit together. It provides the basis for the programme plan critical path, as where a project is dependent on another project, any delays will have knock-on consequences.

Transition plans are basically yours. They are inherently linked to your benefits realization plan. The transition plans cover taking the capability and turning it into the outcomes. The plan is essential to enable business performance control. Ad hoc changes mean that you lose control and it will be harder to maintain control of the 'as-is' state. The Realizing the Benefits process in the transformational flow provides a lot of pointers to help you with this.

'The sooner you fall behind, the more time you have to catch up.' Ogden's Law

9.2 WHAT DOES MSP HAVE TO SAY?

Planning and control are key to the success of any transformation programme and should be seen as distinctly separate concepts and activities.

9.2.1 Programme planning

The preparation of the programme plan involves:

- Processing large amounts of information
- Extensive consultation
- Building the plan.

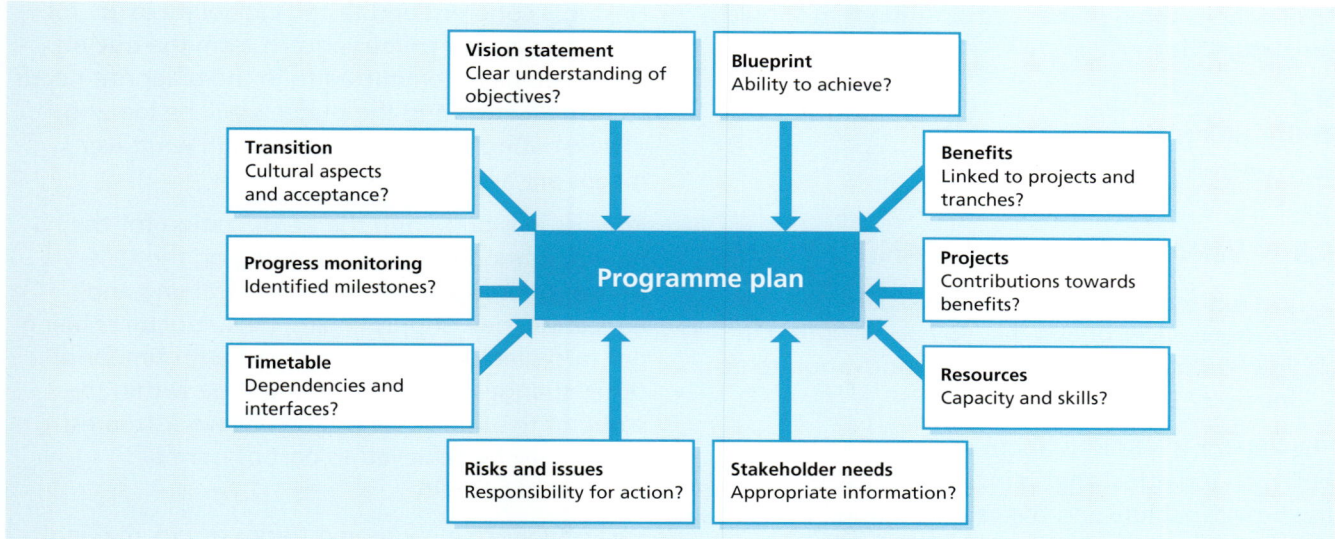

Figure 9.2 Contributions to the programme plan

During its early iterations the programme plan will include many unknowns and a high level of ambiguity.

Figure 9.2 is taken from the MSP guide and shows contributions to the programme plan.

9.2.2   Programme control

Programme control provides supporting activities and processes that run throughout the lifecycle of the programme to:

■ Refine and improve delivery
■ Minimize the impact of ambiguity
■ Bring certainty wherever possible
■ Justify the continuance of the programme.

The management and control of the programme should be based on experiences from the previous tranches.

Programme control should consider and develop:

■ Monitoring and control strategy
■ Dependency management
■ Starting projects
■ Integration of information
■ Progress monitoring
■ Project control
■ Planning and controlling transition.

9.2.3   Transition management

While an estimate of the length of the transition period should be considered when developing the overall programme plan, more detailed transition planning is not practical until sufficient progress has been made in each individual tranche. Detailed transition planning requires both knowledge of the specific project outputs and the state of readiness of the operations which are due to change.

MSP defines three phases of transition that should be planned for:

- Pre-transition
- Transition
- Post-transition.

9.3 WHAT DOES THIS MEAN TO YOU?

'No matter how good you are at planning, the pressure never goes away. So I don't fight it. I feed off it. I turn pressure into motivation to do my best.' Benjamin Carson

The key for the BCM is about maintaining balance between the effort that is invested in delivering the new capability and the rate of change that the organization can absorb.

The focus is making sure that the programme plan fits with the drivers and the requirements of the organization. This may result in demand for faster implementation or there may be reasons why the programme needs to slow down. The timescales and priorities will be driven by the programme board and should reflect the drivers and deadlines for change and the ability to absorb it.

9.3.1 Why is it important to you?

'Think ahead. Don't let day-to-day operations drive out planning.' Donald Rumsfeld

The benefits realization plan may well define how the delivery of promised benefits will happen after the programme completes. The important thing for you to remember is that the programme plan will define how the delivery of the capability (described in the blueprint) will be achieved, so that the outcomes will materialize.

Having a coherent and tested capability ready for transition is your prime concern from the outset. What you have committed to in the blueprint needs to be delivered, and the projects will be looking after creating the capability through whatever means are appropriate.

Your issue is preparing the organization for the new operating model. Depending on the type of programme, this could involve training and education, new supply chains, new structures being put into place, new buildings and any number of other changes. Some of these will be within the scope of the individual projects or workstreams; others may be achieved as part of normal operational activity.

Part of your role is keeping things going, making sure that the capabilities are going to deliver what you need and the organization is preparing for the change.

9.3.1.1 Resource management

An element of planning and control is resource management; the programme manager will develop a strategy and a plan. The challenge for you is to ensure that the strategy covers your needs for transition and organizational support as well as resourcing the needs of the projects.

9.3.2 What do you need to do?

You are responsible for transition planning and when preparing for it you need to be conscious of the tendency towards optimism bias. It is a phenomenon that has come through strongly from P3M3 (Portfolio, Programme and Project Management Maturity Model) assessments; organizations generally have very few standards when it comes to creating plans and they tend to be

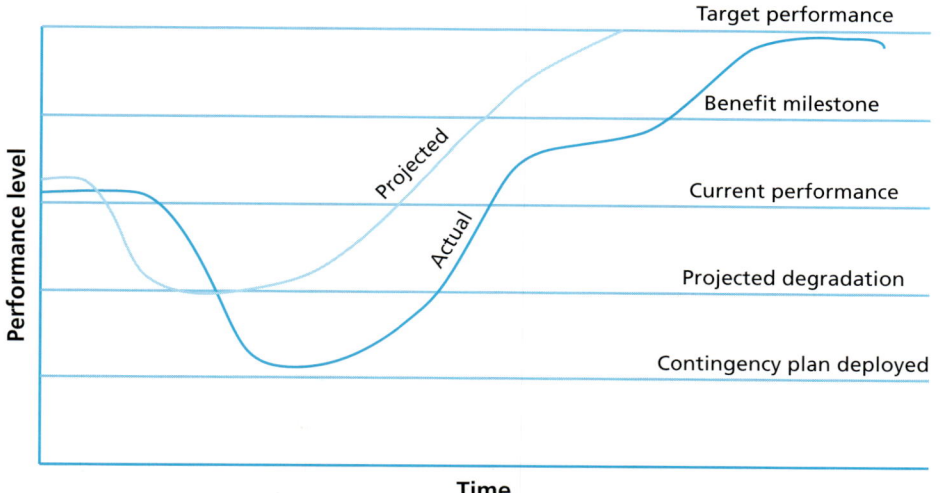

Figure 9.3 Actual versus projected performance

a long list of estimates that are all optimistic. The aggregating effect is that there is this tremendous sense of optimism and later failure comes as a surprise; this happens repeatedly, which is the real surprise.

It is therefore a good strategy on your part to plan like a pessimist to help balance the approach. There is a technique called three-point estimation, where the estimate is based on best-case, worst-case and likely-case scenarios. It would be very worthwhile for you to ensure that there are techniques like that in place for the projects, as it will give you much more confidence in your planning. These would normally be defined in the monitoring and control strategy.

With regard to the control aspects of your role, you need to be carefully watching for any degradation in organizational performance. The programme could have effects long before formal changes happen. These effects could improve or degrade the performance as a result of morale issues or freeing up resources by stopping projects in an emergent programme. Some of the changes may or may not be attributable but you will need to keep aware of developing trends.

The one thing that is sure is that performance will deteriorate during and after transition, so prepare projections of what will happen and when the performance will pick up (see Figure 9.3). A projection such as this sets out the scenario where any contingency plans may need to be deployed.

If the performance varies from the projection then it will give the basis for improving forecasting in the future. If the performance doesn't degrade, it may be an indication that the organization can absorb change better than anticipated. Be careful not to jump to conclusions as there could be other changes going on inside or outside the organization that are having either a positive or negative effect.

Table 9.1 Key roles in planning and control

Role	Area of focus
Senior responsible owner (SRO)	Consulting with the sponsoring group and other key stakeholders, maintaining their buy-in, especially in preparing for and carrying out transition
	Leading the ongoing monitoring and review activities of the programme, mid-tranche and end-of-tranche, including commissioning formal reviews such as audits/health checks, if required
	Monitoring progress and direction of the programme at a strategic level and initiating management interventions where necessary
	Authorizing the resource management strategy
	Authorizing the monitoring and control strategy
	Ensuring that adequate assurance is designed into the control mechanisms
	Authorizing the projects dossier, programme plan, and the required monitoring and control activities
Programme manager	Designing the projects dossier, resource management strategy, monitoring and control strategy and the required assurance activities
	Designing the programme plan
	Ensuring that the blueprint, programme plan, benefits realization plan and benefit profiles are consistent and able to deliver the business case and remain aligned
	Developing the resource management strategy and deployment of the plan
	Developing the monitoring and control strategy and its deployment
	Establishing and managing the appropriate governance arrangements for the programme and its projects
	Ensuring that key programme documentation is current
	Creating and issuing project briefs
	Identifying and managing programme dependencies
	Progress reporting to the SRO and the programme board on project, business case, programme plan and blueprint achievement
	Adjusting the projects dossier, blueprint and plans to optimize benefits realization
	Managing stakeholder expectations and participating in communications activities to inform stakeholders of progress and issues

Role	Area of focus
Business change manager(s)	Consulting with the programme manager on designing the projects dossier, and scheduling the tranches and constituent projects to ensure that the transition will align with the required benefits realization
	Ensuring that changes are implemented in the business
	Ensuring that the business continues to operate effectively during the period of change
	Providing adequate and appropriate business and operational resources to the programme and its projects to ensure that outputs are designed, developed and assured to give them the best chance of enabling the scale of improvements required
	Making sure that operational functions are adequately prepared and ready to change when transition starts
	Ensuring that plans are in place to maintain business operations during the change process until transition and handover is complete; also providing input to the reviews
	Planning the transition within operational areas, accommodating requirements to maintain business operations
	Ensuring that the focus remains once transition is completed, to establish the new ways of working and ensure that old practices do not creep back
Programme office	Supporting the development of planning, control and information management arrangements
	Gathering information and presenting progress reports on projects
	Supporting the programme manager in the development of reports
	Providing the programme teams with information and resources that can assist with the design of documentation
	Establishing and operating the programme's information and configuration management systems, procedures and standards
	Collecting monitoring and measurement data and keeping the information up to date
	Collecting and presenting information on business performance
	Ensuring that there are coherent and common project-level standards in place for all document management arrangements for the programme

9.4 YOUR ROLE IN PLANNING AND CONTROL

It is tempting to see planning and control as the domain of the programme manager; to some extent it is but you need to be heavily involved. The programme manager may well bring technical expertise and experience but you will be bringing the organizational expertise to support them. As with all things in a programme, it is a team effort.

9.4.1 Other BCMs

You and the other BCMs will always be under pressure to deliver change faster and release the benefits sooner. The big issue is maintaining control; to achieve that you first need to have decent plans to work from. Different parts of an organization will be able to transition at different rates. Some will be more adaptable and flexible while others will be more rigid and resistant, but this will probably reflect the nature of their functions. All this will need to be fed into your transition and benefits realization plans.

9.4.2 The SRO

With the SRO your relationship will be about ensuring realism in what the organization can achieve within the timescales. The SRO will be driven by timescales that are often beyond their control and are inflexible. They also have their reputation to protect so they will want ambitious timescales but not impossible ones.

9.4.3 The programme manager

With the programme manager your relationship will be crucial because there is plenty of room for conflict as the demands on your time may be quite different. The programme manager will be under pressure to deliver faster and at a lower cost, while you can't afford to compromise on quality as it may affect the benefits and you may not be able to cope with the rate of change. The blueprint is absolutely vital to your relationship. If you haven't got one then the potential for failure will be much higher. The programme manager is responsible for creating the resource management strategy, and resourcing your BCM team should be included as part of this strategy.

Table 9.1 shows the MSP key roles and areas of focus for planning and control.

The business case

10

10 The business case

'Change will not come if we wait for some other person or some other time. We are the ones we've been waiting for. We are the change that we seek.' Barack Obama

The business case in programme management is the illustration of the justification to make the change. They come in many different shapes and sizes and there is a danger that there is a lot of duplication between the contents of the business case and other documents. The approach is often specific to organizations so this advice has to be generic.

Many organizations see business cases as a necessary evil to be able to get at the funding, and the detail is quickly filed away in File 13 (bottom drawer and hidden from sight) and forgotten about, unless it is produced as evidence later to blame or prove the innocence of someone.

Example

A finance director at a programme board meeting made a telling comment: 'How come we seem to spend months getting to the point where I sign the business case, then we hear nothing from the project for 18 months, at which point I'm told it is 18 months behind schedule and about to go over budget?'

This sums up the approach of many organizations to their business case management.

Another reality is that numbers are often created to fit the justifications. Consequently, the benefits are exaggerated and costs minimized to help the numbers stack up so that the business case can get approval to go ahead.

'Statistics are used much like a drunk uses a lamppost: for support, not illumination.' Vin Scully

10.1 BASIC PRINCIPLES

There are three parts to the business case. Firstly, there are the options that have been identified. One of them should always be 'do nothing' and if you are running a compliance programme, this will give you the justification to change (i.e. avoidance of the penalties for not changing). There should always be at least three reasonable options for the senior responsible owner (SRO) to consider, which means that at least three potential blueprints will need to be developed to enable the analysis.

Secondly, there are the benefits. These have been covered extensively in the benefits management chapter (Chapter 6) and this chapter will focus on the concept of risk-factoring the benefits to ensure they are realistic.

Thirdly, there are the costs. The different blueprints will have different delivery paths and in fact a preferred blueprint may also have a number of delivery options. The business case should include the costs for each of these and the associated level of risks with the estimates. The majority of the costs are associated with the projects.

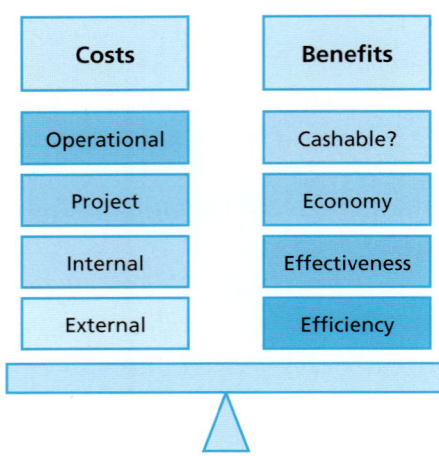

Figure 10.1 Balance of costs and benefits

Figure 10.1 illustrates the balance between the costs and the main types of benefits.

The business case often evolves during the programme. It shouldn't be a document that is created at the end of programme definition to sell the justification for expenditure (which happens in many organizations). It is a concept that is evolving through a number of documents (see Figure 10.2). The programme mandate provides the strategic concept, the programme brief sets out the justification to continue with the work and finally the full business case is produced.

The decision about the right course of action will be based on risk to the organization and the chances of success. The lower-risk approach often produces the lower benefits, but you can't have it all ways.

Once approved, the key review points are at the ends of tranches, when the viability is reassessed and decisions are made to either continue, change direction to one of the other end states, change the preferred delivery approach, or stop.

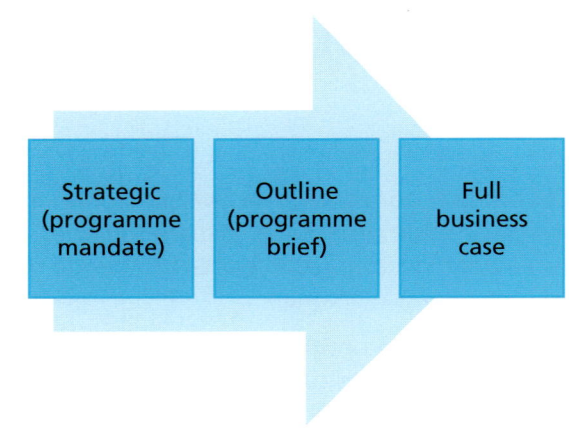

Figure 10.2 Development of the business case

10.2   WHAT DOES MSP HAVE TO SAY?

In MSP the business case provides the vital test of the viability of the programme. It answers the question: 'Is the investment in this programme still worth it?'. It evolves from the early documents (e.g. programme mandate and programme brief), and develops throughout the lifecycle, providing a critical decision-making tool.

It provides more than just the basis for initial approval to start the programme. It is actively maintained throughout the programme, and continually updated with new information on benefits, costs and risks.

The business case presents the optimum 'mix' of information used to judge whether or not the programme is (and remains) desirable, viable and achievable.

Table 10.1 Costs to include in the business case

Type	Description	Possible information source
Project costs, sometimes referred to as investment or development costs	Project costs in acquiring and delivering the enabling outputs	Projects dossier
	For project and programme contingency and change budget	Programme plan
		Project business cases
Benefits realization costs	Setting up and implementing measurement, monitoring, and reporting on benefits realization	Benefits management strategy
	Other costs incurred in achieving the benefits, which can be attributed to benefits – for example, compensation packages for staff	Benefit profiles
		Benefits realization plan
Business change and transition costs	Cost of preparing, training, moving and supporting an operational unit until new practices are embedded. This could include interim operational resources required to embed the change	Programme plan
		Resource management plan
	Costs of activities defined in the Realizing the Benefits element of the tranche, including the costs of the BCM and business change team	Benefit profiles
Programme management costs	Some programme roles will be full time: for example the programme office and the programme manager	Resource management plan
	Associated costs for these roles and for programme management activities: for example office space, programme tools for tracking and reporting progress	Information management strategy
	Contingency budget for dealing with risk and change	Programme communications plan
	Assurance and review costs	Quality and assurance strategy
		Programme plan
Capital costs	Capital costs are normally for fixed assets, which can often be found under the 'technology' heading in the blueprint. In accountancy terms the impact of these costs will often be spread over a number of years	Blueprint

Developing and maintaining the business case includes:

- Genesis of the business case as it gains detail from initial elements in the original programme mandate, to outline business case in the programme brief and then a full business case that is updated as the programme proceeds.
- The business case construction that sets out costs, the benefits realization and the risk profiles, to assess programme viability.

Reviewing the business case should be an ongoing activity by the programme manager, business change manager (BCM) and programme office. It should also be formally validated (reviewed and re-accepted) at the end of each tranche by the programme board and SRO.

Managing the business case is important to check to what extent the programme can realize the expected benefits, and whether changes to the cost–benefit profile would alter the status and relative priority of the programme in relation to meeting the corporate strategic objectives.

Table 10.1 shows costs that should be considered for inclusion in the business case.

10.3   WHAT DOES THIS MEAN TO YOU?

'Experience taught me a few things. One is to listen to your gut, no matter how good something sounds on paper. The second is that you're generally better off sticking with what you know. And the third is that sometimes your best investments are the ones you don't make.'
Donald Trump

The business case is a rather dangerous document for you, and it reflects the difference in roles between yourself and the programme manager. The programme manager spends the money and you produce the benefits, so you should be clear what you are signing up for.

10.3.1   What do you need to do?

'There are two ways of lying. One, not telling the truth and the other, making up statistics.'
Josefina Vazquez Mota

This quotation can be summarized by saying get your facts straight and make sure you can stand behind the numbers in the business case in relation to the cost of change.

It is undoubtedly true that if business cases included the full cost of the organizational change then many of the failures that have happened would never have proceeded. Even the cost of the business change team will be challenged in immature organizations.

The reality of the cost of change should be offset against the benefits, but of course organizations can choose to swallow these costs outside the business case. It is your duty to endeavour to assemble the full cost of the change to the organization.

The programme business case will be based on the aggregated costs of the projects and should include the cost of the programme overhead. As the programme proceeds each project will work to their allotted budget. A project in a programme doesn't have a business case, or if it does it is more in name than a real business case. The project will calculate its costs and how it will contribute to the blueprint and benefits, and the delivery of these are in your remit not the project's.

Example

In 2007, Aspire Europe worked with a client to calculate the true cost of project delivery. It was found that the costs of 45 staff were accounted for in the business cases but research on what resources were actually being used showed that more than 150 staff were being used by operational resources that were not accounted for. In effect, two-thirds of the resources being used were not in the business cases and it helped to explain why the organization was struggling, as its response was to bring in more project people who promptly pulled in more operational staff to help.

A checklist of where costs will be incurred should include:

- Developing requirements and specifications
- Product testing
- Contributing to or reviewing project documentation
- Attendance at project and programme meetings
- Time spent travelling to and from meetings and training events (this is a big one)
- Communication plan activities
- Business change team activities
- Training time
- Responding to correspondence.

The other costs that you are responsible for are any operational cost changes. This is where the benefits are likely to come from but hidden costs in terms of maintenance, warranties and different working practices need to be systematically identified and included in the business case.

Hints and tips

Moving to a leasing model may save capital but it brings with it significant management overhead costs that did not previously exist in terms of management of assets that were once yours but now belong to someone else and you will need to return them.

10.3.2 Why is it important to you?

It is essential to understand the level of risk associated with the achievement of the benefits, as this contributes to understanding the overall level of risk for the programme. The best approach is to associate a numeric value with the level of risk and use this to factor the amount of the benefit that is achievable.

One of the categories for benefits is risk level and assessing the risk level comes in really useful during building of the business case.

The value of benefits will change due to changing environmental events. Some of these are predictable and some are highly volatile. If the level of risk is not taken into consideration when developing the benefit profiles for an initiative, inappropriate expectations can be set for the financial or business plan. Opportunities for greater realization may be missed if there isn't enough recognition of the need for additional effort to exploit an opportunity.

The value that should be attributed to a particular benefit should be factored based on Table 10.2. The decision about how much value to apply will be based on the analysis of the benefit controls later in the document.

Table 10.2 Confidence evaluation

Confidence	Value	Explanation of confidence
Very high	90%	This should only be used if the level of certainty is almost total. It will normally only be achieved with low levels of dependency on other initiatives and in areas where there is direct control of events and where this kind of benefit has been delivered in the past in this way.
Highly likely	75%	This should be used where there is previous experience of achieving a benefit of this kind in this context. There may be areas of ambiguity, possibly with stakeholder commitment, or a small number of dependencies outside the control of the initiative that may affect the total value of the benefits.
Likely	60%	Likely is when, on the balance of probabilities, the majority of the benefit will be achieved. Under the management controls there will be a number of factors that could be positive or could be negative, one of which may be previous experience of delivering this type of change into particular areas.
		The amount of value attributed reflects the element of uncertainty and what you can be sure will actually turn up. This doesn't mean that the outstanding amount of the estimate will not appear, but it is a case of being prudent.
Uncertain	40%	This is where the management controls are highlighting that there are recognized risks to achieving the benefit. These could be for a number of reasons and it reflects your confidence in the ability of the organization to deliver the change and capture the benefits.
		It may also reflect high levels of negative effects that could undermine the positive benefits.
		Where the benefit is 'uncertain' it may highlight that additional effort is required to leverage the opportunity over and above the work of the normal projects and programme team – this effort may not be available or its effectiveness may be limited.
Low likelihood	20%	A low likelihood rating may well reflect that the potential benefit has high levels of ambiguity associated with it which reduces confidence that the value can be delivered.
		This may be reflected in a very high-value benefit which is going to require large-scale organizational change to achieve or may face significant resistance. This will increase the costs and threats to business performance to gain the prize.

Table 10.3 Key roles in the business case

Role	Area of focus
Senior responsible owner (SRO)	Answering to the sponsoring group for the successful delivery of the programme and achievement of the business case
	Securing investment for the programme
	Ensuring that the business case is controlled and audit trails are in place to account for changes as the programme develops
	Scanning the business horizons surrounding the programme for issues that will lead to realignment of the programme in some way
	Ensuring that the progress of the programme remains aligned to the business case
	Consulting with the sponsoring group to identify any early-warning indicators of change that may undermine the business case or cause it to lose strategic alignment
	Initiating independent assurance reviews of business case viability
Programme manager	Preparing the business case
	Supporting the SRO in the ongoing validation and review of the business case
	Managing the programme's expenditure against the overall investment defined in the business case
	Identifying opportunities to optimize the business case
Business change manager(s)	Profiling the benefits and dis-benefits and their associated costs
	Ensuring that benefits continue to be valid through regular business case reviews
	Ensuring that the full cost of change is being captured in the business case
	Identifying operational risks to the business case and ensuring that they are controlled
	Measuring benefits at the start of the programme and tracking throughout to inform the net benefits
	Managing business change costs
	Managing benefits realization costs
	Realizing the profiled benefits
Programme office	Supporting the SRO and the programme manager in compiling and updating the business case
	Collecting and maintaining business case information
	Facilitating business case reviews

10.4   YOUR ROLE AND THE BUSINESS CASE

The responsibilities for the business case are evenly spread around the programme board, and the interfaces with the other members can be summarized as follows.

10.4.1   Other BCMs

The BCMs will have their names against the benefits; some may be spread across different parts of the organization and some may be unique to you. The big thing is that you are clear on what each of you is signing up to and you have a clear line of sight on how and when they will be delivered. By sharing a business change team you should be able to optimize your resources and keep the costs of delivery appropriate. Make sure that your requirements are clearly defined in the blueprint to ensure there is no ambiguity.

10.4.2   The SRO

With the SRO there will need to be transparency and honesty. The business case is the one document on which their performance will be judged. They will want it to be realistic but if the numbers don't stack up they will probably put you under pressure to reassess your costs, which is therefore almost an inevitable part of the process. Remember that if you take costs out of the business case they won't disappear, so you will have a difficult communications job to do in your organization if this happens.

10.4.3   The programme manager

The programme manager will be under the most pressure to get the project and programme costs down and make the numbers stack up. Once the programme starts to roll out they will be focused on budgets and cost tracking. You need to work very closely to support them and also keep an eye out so that there are no shortcuts being taken on the projects to save money which could undermine your benefits and blueprint.

Table 10.3 shows the MSP areas of focus for the key roles.

Quality and assurance management

11

11 Quality and assurance management

'The greatest danger in times of turbulence is not the turbulence – it is to act with yesterday's logic.' Peter Drucker

Quality and assurance aren't the most exciting topics and at first glance there isn't too much for the business change manager (BCM) to worry about as they appear to be the domain of the programme manager and the project teams. But this isn't the case. Assurance can be your guardian angel.

Quality management in a programme is somewhat different from that found in a project, where it is all about testing, compliance and fitness for purpose. At a programme level it is about the quality of the management and the way it interfaces with the environment around it, so it does very much affect you.

The value of assurance has become increasingly recognized in recent years. Research has shown that most programmes and projects that go wrong do so quite early on in their lifecycle, and if this had been spotted then a lot of waste could have been avoided by doing the things right and making tough decisions. So again, this does affect you because you are responsible for the benefits, and they don't happen on unsuccessful programmes.

'Success is the result of perfection, hard work, learning from failure, loyalty, and persistence.' Colin Powell

11.1 BASIC PRINCIPLES

Quality and assurance management are clearly differentiated within MSP; however, they are complementary topics which is why they are considered together.

Quality management looks at how well the programme is being run, and within an MSP programme there are three dimensions: principles, quality and assurance (see Figure 11.1).

Earlier the seven programme management principles that represent the characteristics of successful programmes were explained (see section 2.5.1). Quality management is about making sure that your programme adheres to those principles and as the BCM you will have a particular responsibility for the principles relating to 'Designing and delivering a coherent capability' and 'Focusing on the benefits and threats to them' (see section 2.5.1).

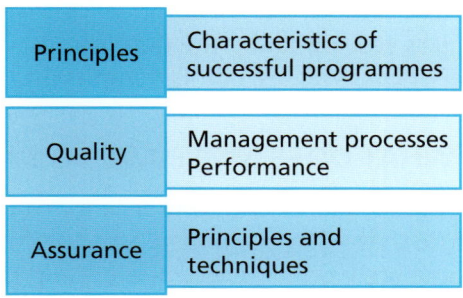

Figure 11.1 The three dimensions of quality management in MSP

The qualities of the management processes that keep the programme under control are critical to success. If they are too heavy they will not be followed and if they are too light there will be inadequate control: each organization is different. The governance themes identify a number of them in the strategies, but there are a few others that need to be considered. In particular: how well is the team managed, rewarded and the skills and capability built and maintained; how strong and effective is the leadership; and how well is the supply chain managed, maintained and used to the programme's advantage.

Assurance, in simple terms, is a regular activity by an independent group whose aim is to provide advice and guidance on how you are performing and advice on ways to optimize the achievement of programme objectives or help to resolve problems. Assurance could be provided by an external expert, peer group or governance body, who review one or more aspects of the programme. You would expect to have assurance reviews of the programme itself, reviews of projects and reviews of business areas that are preparing for or have already changed.

Assurance is different from audit, which is a backwards view to check for compliance. Put simply, audit checks you are doing the right things, while assurance checks you are doing things right.

11.2 WHAT DOES MSP HAVE TO SAY?

The purpose of quality and assurance management is to ensure that all management aspects of the programme are working appropriately and that it stays on target to achieve its objectives. If a programme does not apply quality and assurance effectively to its management activities, then it is less likely to achieve its objectives and deliver the anticipated value and benefits.

Quality and assurance are defined as follows:

- **Quality** is the totality of features and inherent or assigned characteristics of a product, person, process, service and/or system that bears on its ability to show that it meets expectations or stated needs, requirements or specifications.
- **Assurance** is the systematic set of actions necessary to provide confidence to the senior responsible owner (SRO) and stakeholders that the programme remains under control and on track to deliver and that it is aligned with the organization's strategic objectives.

Quality and assurance management must run continuously throughout the life of a programme; achieving the right level of quality must be an integral part of all the day-to-day activities of the programme.

The programme management principles describe the characteristics of a successful programme and act as critical success factors that apply to all programmes. Therefore, application of and adherence to the principles is essential for the programme to achieve a successful conclusion. To this end, the principles act as the focal point for establishing the critical things that the programme must do to be successful, and quality management makes sure that the programme is doing the right things to assure their achievement.

Whereas the programme principles set out the areas that are critical to the success of a programme, the scope of quality is broader. It covers eight process areas that require management review of their effectiveness in supporting the achievement of the programme objectives (see Figure 11.2).

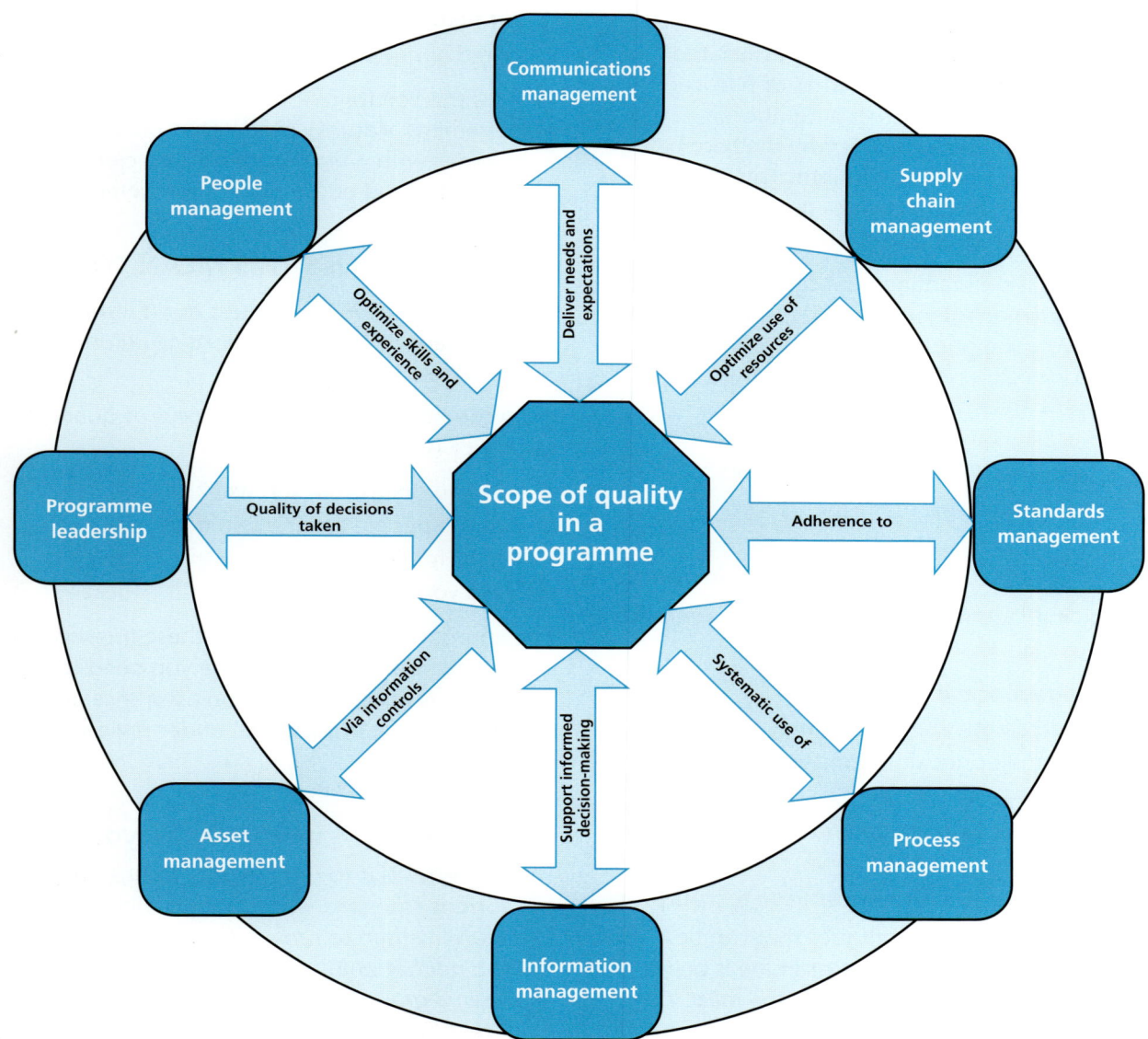

Figure 11.2 Scope of quality in a programme

A number of these processes are covered as part of the MSP governance themes and associated strategies; however, these are areas of particular importance that can cut across a number of themes and strategies, which is why they are being emphasized here in their own right. This is not an exhaustive list, but it provides useful scope for setting out the programme strategy for quality.

The emphasis is on management for all the topics, because good management requires good processes to be in place. The one exception is programme leadership, which is relevant across all the management areas.

11.2.1 Assurance management in a programme

11.2.1.1 Assurance management principles

Assurance management should follow an approach that is:

- Independent of the programme
- Integrated across the programme
- Linked to major decision points
- Risk-based
- Based on follow-up action and intervention.

11.2.1.2 Assurance management techniques

There are a number of techniques that can be used to help assure that the programme is being delivered optimally, that is to say in the most appropriate and effective way for the achievement of its purpose and objectives. These include:

- Audit
- Effectiveness of measurements
- Assurance reviews

- P3M3 maturity assessments
- Gated reviews.

P3M3 is the Portfolio, Programme and Project Management Maturity Model that provides a framework with which organizations can assess their performance and put in place improvement plans.

11.3 WHAT DOES THIS MEAN TO YOU?

'It's fine to celebrate success but it is more important to heed the lessons of failure.'
Bill Gates

From the BCM perspective the focus of quality and assurance is three-fold:

- Are you doing your job well?
- Are the people around you doing their job properly?
- Have your missed anything?

The approach in MSP covers all these questions and at the outset of the programme you need to ensure that there is adequate focus on assurance and a plan to help keep the programme under review and out of trouble.

11.3.1 Why is it important to you?

'Far better is it to dare mighty things, to win glorious triumphs, even though checkered by failure … than to rank with those poor spirits who neither enjoy nor suffer much, because they live in a gray twilight that knows not victory nor defeat.' Theodore Roosevelt

Assurance is your friend, and the less experienced you are the bigger the friends you need. There are some specific areas where you can easily be caught out and where it would be sensible to make use of assurance.

You are responsible for delivering change in what is probably a complex environment. Your enthusiasm and ambition for this change may not be matched by your colleagues or staff. Although they may be nodding and agreeing with everything you say, you need to be assured that when you are being told transition plans are in place and preparations are being made this is actually the case.

Readiness-for-change audits form an important area and an independent review on your behalf will come in very useful from time to time.

Benefits are very volatile and where you are dependent on a chain of events the level of volatility increases and the likely release of benefits will reduce. It is not unusual for reorganizations and other changes to release potential benefits before the programme arrives or to remove the potential to release them. Independent reviews of operational status and performance can check that the status quo has remained and that the original projected benefits still exist.

Reviews of the projected outputs of the projects and how they align with the blueprint are equally important. It is often the case that minor deviations and changes to specifications at the project level combine to undermine elements of the blueprinted outcomes. The result of this is that some fundamental capabilities may be missing, creating significant problems during transition and undermining the ability to release benefits due to functional deficiencies in the capability.

11.3.2 What do you need to do?

The important thing for the BCM is to be proactive and ensure that you plan for assurance.

If you have doubts about what is going on in your own or other BCMs' parts of the organization or the quality and timeliness of the capabilities being developed then you have a justification for instigating assurance reviews so that you know the extent of the issues, or whether you have been worrying unnecessarily.

11.3.3 Assurance approaches

There are a few useful techniques around that cover this. Three of them, all of which represent a form of assurance, are described below.

Health checks are targeted reviews of the whole of a programme, a particular perspective or the performance of a particular group. A health check will need to be scoped and resourced and is intended to be a low-impact method of checking things are being done in the best way.

Maturity assessments look at the whole or part of an organization in terms of maturity of process. These are not normally used for a single programme but would look at how consistently all the programmes are run: without consistency it is difficult to improve. Most are based on the five-level Capability Maturity Model Integration (CMMI). The levels are:

- **Level 1** Awareness of process – ad hoc, chaotic or heroic, but every one is different.
- **Level 2** Repeatable – some are working to a common plan, but others aren't.
- **Level 3** Defined – all programmes are being managed consistently.
- **Level 4** Managed – they are learning from experience and continual improvement is in place.

Table 11.1 Key roles in quality and assurance management

Role	Area of focus
Senior responsible owner (SRO)	Consults with sponsoring group on approach to programme assurance
	Ensures that an adequate assurance regime is in place for all aspects of quality in the programme
	Signs off the quality and information management strategies
	Initiates assurance reviews and audits
	Maintains focus on the programme management principles
Programme manager	Develops and implements the quality and assurance strategy, and then plans and coordinates delivery of outputs from the projects that are fit for the purpose of achieving the desired outcomes and benefits
	Develops and implements the information management strategy and plan
	Initiates assurance reviews of project and supplier performance
	Ensures that lessons learned are implemented
Business change manager(s)	Implements transitioning, realizing and reviewing of benefits from the outputs of the projects
	Initiates assurance reviews of business performance and change readiness
	Ensures that business change lessons learned are implemented
Programme office	Establishes and maintains the programme's quality and assurance plan and ensures the establishment of the appropriate audit, assurance and review processes for the programme in accordance with the quality and assurance strategy
	Establishes and maintains the programme's information management plan and ensures the establishment of the appropriate audit, assurance and review processes for the programme in accordance with the information management strategy
	Provides information to support assurance reviews

■ **Level 5** Optimized – there are embedded behaviours and practices that are continually improving.

A maturity assessment can be useful within a programme where there are many projects running, so they can be tested for consistency. Where many areas are going through change, a change maturity assessment can check that the lessons are being learned and there is a consistent approach. Level 3 is a good place to be for most organizations.

Gated reviews are often approached with trepidation as they are auditing progress. They are also the BCM's best friend because they will identify issues you may not know about. They are a very good place to confess your sins or concerns and share doubts, as the reports are normally non-attributable, but you might want to check that before saying too much.

11.4 YOUR ROLE IN QUALITY AND ASSURANCE MANAGEMENT

When it comes to quality and assurance, you may well have a lower-profile role than the other players.

11.4.1 The SRO

The SRO will be concerned with the overall state of the programme and whether it is going to meet its objectives. There is often more focus on the projects and whether the money is being spent on the right things in the right places. More enlightened SROs will have their eye on benefits and change management, so it is important that you have a transparent relationship with them and they know the issues you are facing and the potential opportunities.

11.4.2 The programme manager

The programme manager is responsible for running the programme to the standards that are set in the governance strategies and ensuring that the quality and assurance management plan is delivered. The focus of the programme manager is likely to be on the effectiveness of the way that the programme is managing the projects and the programme team, and you may be a little bit off the radar. You need to make sure this doesn't happen as you are the customer for the programme and have to deliver performance improvements. You should be involved in the scrutiny of the projects as you are dependent on them delivering on time and with the right capabilities.

11.4.3 Other BCMs

The other BCMs should seek to have the same reviews highlighted for you. You will often have dependencies on their changes happening in the right way and at the right time to support your own changes, so you need assurance that they are on track too.

Table 11.1 shows the MSP areas for focus for the key roles.

PART 3
The transformational flow

Introduction to the transformational flow

12

12 Introduction to the transformational flow

The transformational flow in MSP, which was introduced in Chapter 2 (see Figures 2.3 and 2.4), is the programme lifecycle. This is where all the action happens; the governance themes are active in all the processes and all the concepts covered in the governance themes come to life.

To help focus the mind on the role of the business change manager (BCM), in Figure 12.1 some of the process activities have been adjusted to bring some sequence to what is happening and also to give you clear and concise advice on where to put your energy. This different view of the lifecycle shows the sequential nature of the processes in the transformational flow.

Managing the Tranches recurs depending on the number of tranches you decide to have. Realizing the Benefits runs concurrently throughout the lifecycle and is your main area of focus; you manage all the activities in this process. The other processes are largely the domain of the programme manager but with you working closely with them.

The processes are covered in more detail in Chapters 13 to 18.

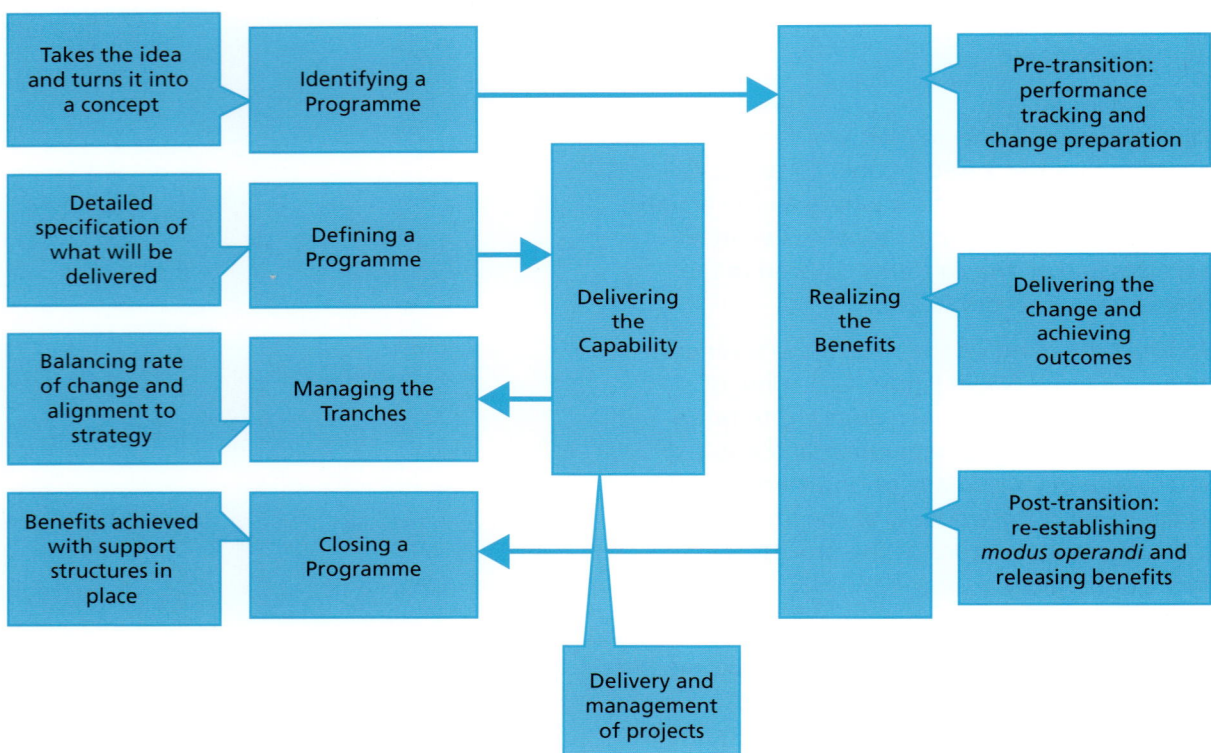

Figure 12.1 Sequential view of transformational flow

Identifying a Programme

13 Identifying a Programme

'Change does not change tradition, it strengthens it. Change is a challenge and an opportunity.' Prince Phillip

Identifying a Programme is the process that kicks off the programme and you need to get involved nice and early. Your role begins with the formation of the programme board, which reflects the need to have you involved from the start.

There are many programmes that don't ever come out of identifying because they sort out a vision and, before you know it, there are projects being launched all over the place and the blueprint and benefits go missing. Instead of a programme there is a cluster of projects with no particular context.

Try to make sure that there is a programme brief and there is focus on outcomes and benefits from the start. There must be recognition that you need to go through a formal Defining a Programme process and that the appearance of the programme brief isn't the job done, as so often happens.

13.1 WHAT DOES MSP HAVE TO SAY?

Identifying a Programme comprises a number of activities that take an initial or emerging idea or need and frame it into a tangible concept that the business can support through the Defining a Programme process.

13.1.1 Activities

1 Sponsor the programme

2 Confirm the programme mandate

3 Appoint the senior responsible owner (SRO) and programme board

4 Produce the programme brief

5 Develop the programme preparation plan

6 Independent review

7 Approval to proceed (with Defining a Programme).

13.2 RECOMMENDED ACTIONS

Identifying a Programme is the first process in the programme lifecycle, and at the outset the programme is likely to have a lot of ambiguity about what is required.

The activities in Identifying a Programme should seek to put context around the programme, clarify its organizational context, develop the outline vision for the programme and establish a strong team to undertake further development.

The result of these activities may well be a decision not to proceed with the programme: this is OK, as it is much better to stop it early before time and effort are expended on a programme that is unlikely to proceed. Table 13.1 shows the recommended actions by the BCM for the activities in this process.

Table 13.1 Recommended actions for the BCM in Identifying a Programme

Activity	Recommended actions
Develop the programme brief	The business changes identified are going to be your responsibility, along with the benefits, so ensure that the changes are realistic and that you can sign up to them. There is a risk that the programme begins to gain momentum and unrealistic expectations are set about what benefits can be achieved and the level of change that can be absorbed. Being cautious in what you can commit your organization to achieving is important.
Develop the programme preparation plan	You will need to provide resources (including your own time) to help with this process. This is going to have a significant impact, as it is very much about modelling how the business works now, how it will work in the future and the benefits from the change. You need to be confident that you have the right resources and that they will be available to do this work.
	The existence of the programme preparation plan is essential to ensuring the resources and time are invested in sorting out the blueprint and benefits.
Arrange an independent assurance review	This will be your opportunity to flag up concerns you may have about the realism of the approach. Organizations invariably overestimate their ability to change, which leads to over-optimism in planning for change and benefits and the resultant failure to live up to expectations.
	Is it clear how much resource your organization is being asked to dedicate, and will you be in a position to provide it? Your role is almost entirely focused at delivering this change, so if you have reservations now is the best time to raise them – the programme will start to pick up momentum after this point.
Gain authorization to proceed	You are now signing up to developing the operational changes and benefits outlined in the programme brief. It is important that you liaise with your sponsor on the sponsoring group; you are a key source of advice to them on this decision. You should also ensure that you have had a one-to-one discussion with the SRO so that they know about your views.

Defining a
Programme

14

14 Defining a Programme

'The rate of change is not going to slow down anytime soon. If anything, competition in most industries will probably speed up even more in the next few decades.' John P. Kotter

Defining a Programme can be a drawn-out and frustrating period as you try to answer more questions than you have answers for. However, failure to work through this process systematically is only storing up trouble for the future.

The problem is that the rate of change that is required often dazzles people to the need for thoroughness; the reward is normally reaped in programme failure, when the instigators of the undue haste are long gone.

There will be a desire to get the projects moving. An option that often works is to have your resources working on the blueprint and benefits and ensuring projects that are launched have clear requirements that you have drawn from the blueprint, and that the blueprint develops in parallel with the project design and development.

There are two distinct parts to Defining a Programme: the first part is defining where you are going and why, while the second part is designing how you are going to get there under control.

To help you with this, the MSP Defining a Programme process has been split into two stages, 'Defining the Future Organization' and 'Designing the Programme Delivery', and later in this chapter you will find more detailed sequences of events to help you with these two stages.

14.1 WHAT DOES MSP HAVE TO SAY?

Defining a Programme takes the concept that evolved during Identifying a Programme and develops a compelling business proposition that gains the commitment of the sponsoring group and stakeholders.

The business case and governance for the programme will be developed. The governance defines the strategies for quality, information, stakeholders, risks and issues, benefits, resources, monitoring and control. The various programme approaches contained in the strategies, plans and schedules (covering risk management, communications, benefits realization, resources, quality etc.) are developed to provide information on the resources, dependencies and timescales for delivery and realization of benefits.

A key activity is the development of the blueprint and the investigation of the options available, and the options for delivery.

The inevitable trade-off between resources, costs, quality, timings and benefits requires agreement between the sponsoring group and senior responsible owner (SRO). At the completion of Defining a Programme, formal approval is required from the sponsoring group and SRO to proceed with the programme.

Table 14.1 Recommended actions for the BCM in Defining the Future Organization

Activity	Recommended actions
Establish the team to define the programme	You should ensure you are clear about your role and release time from your normal role to deliver the work. You will now be expected to release the resources from the business to support the programme. This may be challenging, but if you don't have a strong change team then your role will become much more difficult.
Engage key stakeholders	You will know who the stakeholders are, and have valuable information on their concerns and aspirations. This should be shared with the programme manager and you are in a very good position to validate the stakeholder profiles. You are a key communications channel, as your profile and track record should be used to gain the attention of your colleagues and managers.
Refine the vision statement	You should be comfortable that the vision statement fits the needs of your organization or sector, which may or may not be mentioned explicitly. It will be your job to deliver the end state that is being defined. If it is too unrealistic it is better to say so now. The vision should also provide you with enough context to enable you to develop the blueprint and the benefits. It has been known for people to mistake the vision for a blueprint.
Align existing projects	You will need to do an impact analysis on the consequences of losing projects from your short-term business requirements and needs. Sacrifices will need to be made and it may be a good opportunity to create a point beyond which no further work will be done on certain projects in your business areas.
Develop the blueprint	You will be responsible for sourcing a lot of business performance and process information on how things work at the moment: the final blueprint will be the design of how your part of the business will operate in the future.
Develop the benefit profiles	You will need to develop the benefits from the work you did on the blueprint. The assessments must be realistic and achievable; it is better to under-promise and over-deliver. You will be responsible for delivering these benefits within your business, so make sure the estimates are realistic. Make sure that the risks are being captured, particularly those that may reduce the size of the benefit or may be double-counted.
Identify tranches	If the tranches can be aligned with a strategic business plan commitment or to leverage or avoid certain events, this is the opportunity to do it. You need to look carefully at the benefits opportunities associated with these step changes.
Define the projects dossier	You should satisfy yourself that these projects will deliver the capabilities you need for the benefits. Any gaps are the risks that need to be noted. You should also be thinking about non-project activities that will need to be scheduled for your benefits.

Activity	Recommended actions
Appraise the options	You will be a key player in this; ensure you balance the needs of the programme with the needs of your business. You should be looking to keep your SRO informed of progress and consult them as part of the appraisal process. The main considerations are: ■ Considering different future designs (blueprint) ■ Assessing different ways to deliver the future organization ■ Which options are particularly risky ■ Which options produce the best benefits. The best mix is the ratio of time, cost and risk versus the benefits. If an unacceptable business case is emerging, your options are to: ■ Produce a different blueprint ■ Find a different and cheaper way to deliver (projects) ■ Stop the programme.
Plan for the Designing the Programme Delivery phase	You may need to provide resources to help with the next phase; can you afford to spare them? You will be starting to monitor business performance, so check that the plan includes an allowance for these resources.
Arrange an independent review	This will be your opportunity to flag up concerns you may have about the realism of the approach and, in particular, any concerns you may have regarding the benefits and level of business change being planned.
Gain approval to proceed	You are now signing up to begin the process of delivering the benefits and managing the change. You should ensure that you have had one-to-one reviews with the SRO and your sponsoring group executive so they understand your private and public concerns.

14.1.1   Activities

1   Establish the infrastructure for Defining a Programme
2   Establish the team to define the programme
3   Identify and analyse the stakeholders
4   Refine the vision statement
5   Develop the blueprint
6   Develop the benefit profiles
7   Model and refine the benefits
8   Validate the benefits
9   Design the projects dossier
10 Identify tranches
11 Design the programme organization
12 Develop the governance arrangements
13 Develop the programme plan
14 Develop and confirm the programme business case
15 Consolidate the programme definition
16 Prepare for first tranche
17 Approval to proceed.

14.2   RECOMMENDED ACTIONS

The recommended actions for the BCM are linked to the modified activities from MSP to reflect the change of skills and experience needed for the different elements.

14.2.1   Defining the Future Organization

In the first stage of the process the detail in the programme brief is expanded and develops the scenarios and options that the business should consider to solve the challenge. Table 14.1 shows the recommended actions for this stage.

The main information developed during this process is:

- The blueprint or target operating model which the programme will create
- Clear understanding of the benefits that will come from the change
- The step changes in capability that will be produced at various stages of the programme lifecycle and the projects required to deliver them.

14.2.2   Designing the Programme Delivery

By now you should have clarity about where you are going, and this stage will develop the governance controls that will keep the programme on track. Table 14.2 shows the recommended actions for this stage.

Once this stage is completed, the programme will have:

- A fully defined business case
- An organizational structure for the delivery
- A set of strategies for maintaining control during delivery
- A programme plan.

Table 14.2 Recommended actions for the BCM in Designing the Programme Delivery

Activity	Recommended actions
Establish the team	You should ensure you are clear about your role and are releasing time from your normal role to deliver to the programme and your personal objectives. If you can find good operational resources to join the team, it will help in establishing awareness and momentum for the change.
Design the projects dossier	The projects need to be aligned to what you need to deliver in terms of benefits and transition; therefore it is essential that you are satisfied that the projects dossier is adequate for your needs.
Design the programme organization	It is important that you have eyes and ears in the projects as well as embedded in the operations through the business change team. These are not full-time roles but are essential for giving you the intelligence you will need to deliver your objectives.
Develop governance arrangements	This is largely programme manager territory, but you must be comfortable that your needs will be met by these arrangements. Your role is a key element of the governance arrangements and each strategy should define how you and your part of the business will contribute and the role of your change team.
Develop the programme plan	It is critical that enough time is allowed for transition and that realistic benefits realization timescales are in place; commitments made now will be expected to be kept once you move into delivery.
Finalize definition documentation	Your role will require you to sign off this fully defined programme and communicate it to your SRO. Ensure that you understand all aspects and don't be blinded by detail; this is where the devil lurks.
Undertake business impact assessment	Do you have the resources to deliver the change and the support of your organization? It would be good to check that the key decision makers appreciate the extent of the changes and support it.
Finalize the business case	Check that there is clarity between cashable and non-cashable savings and the current estimates are fully reflected with sensitivity ratings included. You are a key signatory of this document and you are committing your organization to the benefits defined.
Prepare for first tranche	You will now need to provide the resources for the business change team to support you in being effective; the plan must cover this. There may be a bigger focus on projects just at this moment, but you and the change team can't afford to let the momentum of the launch leave you at odds with the programme.
Arrange an independent review of design	This will be your opportunity to flag up concerns you may have about the realism of the approach and, in particular, any concerns you may have regarding the benefits and level of business change being planned.
Gain approval to proceed	You are now signing up to deliver the operational changes and benefits for your part of the business – a very big moment for everyone.

Managing the Tranches

15

15 Managing the Tranches

'Culture does not change because we desire to change it. Culture changes when the organization is transformed – the culture reflects the realities of people working together every day.' Frances Hesselbein

Managing the Tranches consists of the process and activities which keep the balance between the rate of potential change being delivered by projects and the ability of the organization to absorb that change.

The activities are designed to ensure that controls are in place and working. They also focus on ensuring that the programme remains aligned to the organization's strategic direction.

Major problems with projects and benefits realization are managed at this level; this is where you will escalate issues that arise in your own process, which is Realizing the Benefits.

This chapter deviates a bit from the activities that MSP recommends. This is because a lot of the MSP activities are related to the specific governance themes and, unlike the early process stages, the activities are continual rather than sequential. The sequence of activities outlined here will help you to be more focused.

15.1 WHAT DOES MSP HAVE TO SAY?

The purpose of the Managing the Tranches process is to implement the defined programme management governance strategies for the programme, ensure that the capability delivery is aligned to the strategic direction of the organization, and enable the release of benefits. This accepts that, as the programme progresses, the process will need to be adapted and refined to assure the effective delivery of the tranches and the final outcomes.

A key principle of the Managing the Tranches process is to maintain the balance between the rate of change being offered by the Delivering the Capability process and the rate of change that the operational areas can cope with. This is managed through the Realizing the Benefits stage, which aligns the programme with the evolving and changing strategic needs of the organization.

Unlike some of the activities in other processes, which tend to happen in a logical sequence, the activities in Managing the Tranches may recur or happen concurrently. Most of the activities are linked to the governance themes and are intended to trigger the cycles. For example, you do not 'manage risk and issues' once: this is a day-to-day activity that occurs throughout the tranche.

Table 15.1 Recommended actions for the BCM in Managing the Tranches

Activity	Recommended actions
Establish the programme delivery team	You will principally be focused on recruiting the change teams and putting the structures in place. Finding good change people will not be easy, so you will need to balance the need for internal knowledge of the business operations with the external expertise of professional change managers.
Establish the governance control framework	Your authority should be embedded within the controls and you need to be comfortable that you will be consulted on key decisions and will be in a position to affect the decisions for the benefit of your business area. You should ensure that the business monitoring and performance information is sufficiently reliable to ensure you are able to control the rate and direction of change.
Mobilize project delivery	You should be taking an active interest in the initiation of projects and signing off project design and delivery documents to ensure they meet your requirements. You should also be ensuring that you have reliable representation on the project boards and steering groups.
Manage programme governance framework	Your key focus should be on preparing the organization for change by ensuring effective stakeholder engagement, monitoring the business stability and ensuring that the future state for the organization is achievable and desirable. The governance framework should be providing you with the information to enable your decision-making and identify problems.
Manage project delivery	You should stay in close contact with the business representatives on the various project boards or steering groups to ensure you are maintaining your intelligence about what the operational issues are. You should also be actively preparing the business for the changes that the projects will be delivering for you.
Manage business performance	This is very much your responsibility. You must have a good intelligence system that is giving you early-warning indicators of business performance going outside acceptable deviation. Stakeholder conflict is inevitable, but it should remain within the anticipated risk levels. It is important that the reporting processes are accurate and that you have a rollback position if things start to go wrong. Most of all, the business change managers will need courage to lead the changes.
Review and refine the programme direction	This will be your opportunity to flag up concerns you may have about the realism of the approach and, in particular, any concerns you may have regarding the benefits and level of business change being planned. If the blueprint is proving unachievable or the benefits can't be delivered, now is the time to speak up.
Review and refine the programme governance framework	From the business perspective, you should consider whether you have had enough influence on the direction and day-to-day decision-making in the programme. If not, now is the time to look for changes.
Plan for next tranche	You may need to reinforce the change team to support you in being effective; the plan must cover this.
Conduct an end-of-tranche review	You are now signing up to deliver the operational changes and benefits for your part of the business for the next tranche; re-establishing your terms of reference and the commitment to your role would be a reasonable request for you to make.

15.1.1 Activities

1 Establish the tranche
2 Direct work
3 Manage risks and issues
4 Control and delivery of communications
5 Undertake audits and assurance reviews
6 Maintain alignment between programme blueprint and business strategy objectives
7 Maintain information and asset integrity
8 Manage people and other resources
9 Procurement and contracts
10 Monitor, report and control
11 Transition and stable operations
12 Prepare for next tranche
13 End-of-tranche review and close.

15.2 RECOMMENDED ACTIONS

Table 15.1 shows the recommended actions by the BCM for the activities in this process.

Delivering the Capability

16

16 Delivering the Capability

'The world hates change, yet it is the only thing that has brought progress.' Charles Kettering

Generally, Delivering the Capability is the domain of the programme manager and the project teams, but you should emphasize your role as the customer for most of this process and as such, you cannot afford to be too hands-off.

The steps below are slightly modified from the MSP guide to make your involvement a little clearer.

16.1 WHAT DOES MSP HAVE TO SAY?

The Delivering the Capability process covers the activities for coordinating and managing project delivery according to the programme plan. Delivery from the projects dossier provides the new outputs that enable the capabilities described in the blueprint. The activities of Delivering the Capability are repeated for each tranche of the programme.

This process delivers the capability defined in the blueprint through the projects defined in the projects dossier. The detail in the blueprint provides the input requirements for the projects, which adopt the strategic requirements and undertake detailed specification and design to deliver the outputs that create the capability needed to achieve the outcomes and deliver the benefits.

16.1.1 Activities

1   Start projects
2   Engage stakeholders
3   Align projects with benefits realization
4   Align projects with programme objectives
5   Governance: manage and control delivery:
   ● Monitor and control progress
   ● Manage risks and control issues
6   Close projects.

16.2 RECOMMENDED ACTIONS

This process is the one which covers the launch, control and delivery of the projects within the programme.

The programme-level activities are relatively light touch and the main controls are within the project management method (which is defined in the monitoring and control strategy). Table 16.1 shows the recommended actions by the BCM for this process.

Table 16.1 Recommended actions for the BCM in Delivering the Capability

Activity	Recommended actions
Commission projects from project register	Although projects are not necessarily your main focus, you may find yourself acting as senior responsible owner or, more likely, ensuring your voice is being heard on the project board by either attending or nominating a representative. Your key area of interest is ensuring that the projects are focused on delivering the capability you need to deliver change. Poor project delivery will undermine your efforts to deliver change. You are also involved in the timetable for delivery of any products which will be used in transition activities and aligning these to any constraints from operations.
Authorize project initiation	Your main focus will be ensuring that the projects will deliver the capability you need to make the changes and release the benefits. You may also incur additional operational costs as a result of the projects. It is therefore essential that you sign off the project documentation to confirm you are happy.
Control project direction	The key area for you to monitor is the blueprint and the benefits to make sure the projects are delivering what you need. You should have business representatives within the projects; you will need to stay in touch with them to make sure you are up to date with the important elements. Your transition and benefits realization timetables need to be synchronized with the progress of the projects.
Set up project assurance reviews	Your primary focus must be on the timing of the delivery of the outputs and the transition arrangements within the business. Your pre-transition arrangements should now be under way and aligned with the delivery expectations of the projects.
Authorize project closure	You may well be taking on operational responsibility for the service changes that the projects have delivered and any supplier relationships or contracts. You need to be fully comfortable that the projects have delivered the functionality you require to deliver the benefits; any additional work should be highlighted as part of closure. Your focus should now turn to maintaining momentum and securing the improvements and increasing performance or amending the benefit profiles to reflect the capability that will not be available.
Undertake a post-implementation review for each project	Your input to this will be crucial. You should be delivering operational improvements as a result of the projects. If they are not happening then there needs to be clarity about why. It may be that the scale of change has been underestimated or estimates on benefits have been weak, or there may have been more opportunities than had been forecast. The results of each review need to be factored into forecasts for other projects and benefits.

Realizing the Benefits

17 Realizing the Benefits

'Change is hard because people overestimate the value of what they have and underestimate the value of what they may gain by giving that up.'
James Belasco and Ralph Stayer

The Realizing the Benefits process is for you as it covers where and when you do the things that were outlined in the governance themes. It starts the day you join the programme board and works through to the point where the programme closes, so this is what your role is all about.

17.1 WHAT DOES MSP HAVE TO SAY?

The purpose of the Realizing the Benefits process is to manage the benefits from their initial identification to their successful realization. The activities cover monitoring the progress of the projects to ensure that the outputs are fit for purpose and can be integrated into operations such that the benefits can be realized.

Realizing the Benefits incorporates the planning and management of the transition from old to new ways of working and the achievement of the outcomes, while ensuring that the operational stability and performance of the operations are maintained. The activities of this process are repeated as necessary for each tranche of the programme.

Three distinct sets of activities are covered in this chapter:

■ **Manage pre-transition** The analysis, preparation and planning for business transformation

■ **Manage transition** Delivering and supporting the changes
■ **Manage post-transition** Reviewing progress, measuring performance and adapting to change.

17.1.1 Activities

1   Manage pre-transition – the analysis, preparation and planning for business transformation:
   ● Establish benefits measurements
   ● Monitor benefits realization
   ● Plan transition
   ● Communicate the change
   ● Assess the readiness for change
2   Manage transition – delivering and supporting the changes:
   ● Initiate transition
   ● Establish support arrangements
   ● Enact transition
   ● Review transition
   ● Manage outcome achievement
3   Manage post-transition – reviewing progress, measuring performance and adapting to change:
   ● Measure benefits
   ● Remove access to legacy working practices and systems
   ● Respond to changing requirements
   ● Monitor and report benefits realization

Table 17.1 Recommended actions for the BCM in Realizing the Benefits

Activity	Recommended actions
Establish and track performance	This is your home territory and you need to keep up to date with what's going on. You will need to decide what metrics are still relevant and look for additional ones to support your monitoring.
Mobilize the change	You will be at the vanguard of this activity. It is specifically your job to champion the change and mobilize the structure of the organization for the changes ahead. This will be a challenging time for you, and therefore you must have the confidence of your colleagues and the hierarchy who need to support you.
Plan for transition	Most of the activities in the plan will belong to you; ensure that you have enough capacity to cover the workload that is being planned and that sufficient resources are being provided to make sure the business remains sustainable.
Assess readiness to change	This is your last chance to prevent potential disaster hitting your operation, so be robust in checking that: ● There is clarity about roles and that adequate training has been undertaken to enable people to deliver their responsibilities ● You are happy with the back-out plans ● You are happy with the communications arrangements and that they are adequate to support you ● You are happy with the handover arrangements ● Additional operational resources to help with the transition are going to be available.
Initiate transition	You are going to be at the front line of this change, supported by the change team. You will need to be actively engaged with the operational leads to ensure they are mobilizing. Your other key focus will be on business performance information and matching actual performance against projections. You will also need to be using the communications channels and resources to the maximum to help get your message across.
Enact transition	Your focus will be on maintaining the focus and momentum within the operational environment. It is crucial that you use your forecast changes in performance to underpin your decision-making. Things will go wrong and there will be performance degradation but these should have been forecast. Keep an eye out in case there are deviations that are so far from this forecast that you need to implement the back-out plans. You need to be careful that you maintain some emotional detachment that ensures there is effective analysis and decision-making in place.
Manage outcome achievement	You should be cautious about business operations being dependent on the project teams. If the transition lasts too long, the teams can end up being part of business as usual, while finishing too early can leave you exposed as you haven't gained the experience. You may now need to oversee the operational handover of services and contracts into operations. This is a period when the momentum for savings can be lost through lack of real understanding of the contractual levers. Your benefits focus should be on understanding the current business performance issues and identifying clear requirements that you can provide to the programme team to help ensure your benefits are going to be secured.

Activity	Recommended actions
Manage additional requirements	There will be plenty with their hands up for a better world and some who think they deserve additional features for the pain they have suffered with the new ways of working! In that context, you will need to provide a filtration system to ensure unreasonable requirements are not being fed into the programme. Some requirements may be better delivered through tactical local changes rather than through projects.
Report benefits achievement	You should be focusing on the performance trends and making doubly sure that your declaration of benefits being achieved is appropriate. It is important that you check the data and, if possible, look for secondary evidence to show that not only the short-term achievements but also the longer-term direction of travel has been established. You also need to be very careful that there is no double-counting of benefits that could undermine the entire credibility of the programme.

17.2 RECOMMENDED ACTIONS

This process is about more than just realizing the actual benefits. It focuses on the change lifecycle and runs throughout the programme lifecycle.

It covers pre-transition, transition and of course post-transition. It is post-transition where the benefits are realized. If the earlier activities are not carried out effectively then benefits will not be achieved. The recommended actions for the business change manager are shown in Table 17.1.

Closing a
Programme

18

18 Closing a Programme

'Think twice before you speak, because your words and influence will plant the seed of either success or failure in the mind of another.'
Napoleon Hill

There is a temptation to shut the door, turn the lights out and evaporate if things haven't gone too well; however, there will normally be positives to come out of even the worst programmes. Part of the reason that research into benefits claims that many benefits are not delivered is because there is a lack of a structured closure to programmes, so the positive effects are not recorded.

In the sections below the MSP activities for this process have been simplified a little so that the guidance is clearer and more specific for your role.

18.1 WHAT DOES MSP HAVE TO SAY?

The purpose of Closing a Programme is to ensure the 'end goal' of formally recognizing that the programme is completed. This is when the programme has delivered the required new capabilities described in the blueprint, and has assessed the outcomes via benefit measures.

18.1.1 Activities

1 Confirm ongoing support is in place
2 Confirm programme closure
3 Notify programme is about to close
4 Review programme
5 Update and finalize programme information
6 Provide feedback to corporate governance
7 Disband programme organization and supporting functions.

18.2 RECOMMENDED ACTIONS

This process covers the structured closure of the programme. This is when defeat can be snatched from the jaws of victory if it is not delivered effectively.

Lessons learned and formal handover of documentation and services characterize a successful closure. The recommended actions for the business change manager are shown in Table 18.1.

Table 18.1 Recommended actions for the BCM in Closing a Programme

Activity	Recommended actions
Initiate programme closure	Your main area of concern is going to be focusing on how the momentum for change is to be sustained when the new services are passed into the operational environment. Clear ownership for maintaining the benefits trajectory will need to be allocated to operational areas, and ideally embedded in their objectives. Where new services or supply arrangements have been put into place, it is essential that there is a planned and structured handover of contracts and contract management arrangements to your business areas.
Enact programme closure	Your main focus will be on taking on the management of new contracts and suppliers. Much of the benefits ownership will be transitioning to you and your delivery colleagues. A major inheritance from the programme should be better management information and performance monitoring tools. These need to be harnessed and built into longer-term business improvement plans which have clear ownership.

Appendix A:
Information summary

Appendix A: Information summary

Programmes generate lots and lots of information and it can be difficult to work out how to link it all together.

The information can be grouped into 'baselines', which are sets of information that are related to each other. Table A.1 shows the information baselines from MSP.

Table A.2 is a summary of the documents which MSP refers to and their purpose and relevance to you as a business change manager. MSP is quite specific in saying these documents are a set of information so you can amalgamate them in the most appropriate way to meet your own needs.

Table A.1 Information baselines

Information baseline	Summary
Boundary	Those that set out the direction and the scope of the programme and as such are the first information set to be created. Contents include: ● Vision statement ● Blueprint ● Benefits information ● Projects information ● Decision document created during the lifecycle (e.g. the programme brief).
Governance	Those that set the standards and frameworks within which the programme will be delivered; they define 'how' the programme will be managed. The areas that need to be covered are the strategies for how the programme will manage: ● Stakeholders ● Resources ● Risk ● Issues ● Quality and assurance ● Internal monitoring and control ● Organization structure ● Benefits ● Information.
Management	Those that are created and used to manage the delivery of the programme; they define 'what' activities will be undertaken by 'whom' to deliver the programme. The information in these may be changing on a daily basis so the baseline is more difficult to maintain and may need to be updated on a regular timeline (e.g. quarterly) but it does need to remain under control. The main areas that are covered in this baseline are the: ● Plans (e.g. programme plan) ● Registers (e.g. risk and issue) ● Profiles (e.g. stakeholders).

Table A.2 Business change manager involvement with MSP documents

Title	Purpose	Why is it important to you?
Benefit profile	Used to define each benefit (and dis-benefit) and provide a detailed understanding of what will be involved and how the benefit will be realized	This is the detailed analysis that you create to develop where and how the benefit will be delivered. You write this one.
Benefits management strategy	Defines the approach to Realizing the Benefits and the framework within which benefits realization will be achieved	This is the framework that defines the boundary and approach to manage benefits in your programme. You write this one.
Benefits map	Illustrates the sequential relationship between benefits	This is your document and results from your first analysis of the benefits. You create this one.
Benefits realization plan	Used to track realization of benefits across the programme and set review controls	This is the plan that shows where and when the changes will happen and who will produce them. You provide the detail but the programme manager tracks it as it is part of programme governance.
Blueprint	Used to maintain focus on delivering the required transformation and business change	You provide the detailed description of the capability that is going to be delivered. The programme manager writes it, but you provide most of the detail.
Business case	Used to validate the initiation of the programme and the ongoing viability of the programme	This is the document where you are signing up to the benefits you will deliver and the costs that your organization is happy to incur. The programme manager writes this.
Information management plan	Sets out the timetables and arrangements for implementing and managing the information management strategy	This is the schedule for where and when information will be created and how the management controls will be applied. The programme manager writes this.

Table continues

Table A.2 *continued*

Title	Purpose	Why is it important to you?
Information management strategy	Describes the measures, systems and techniques that will be used to maintain and control programme information	This sets out how the quality of information will be managed in the programme; it is of interest to you because you will provide a lot of performance information and benefits tracking. The programme manager writes this.
Issue management strategy	Used to describe the mechanisms and procedures for resolving issues	Sets out the framework for managing issues; you need to ensure that it covers operational issues and appropriate escalation routes. The programme manager creates this.
Issue register	Used to capture and actively manage the programme issues	This is where you will be reviewing all the known problems in the programme that could affect your change and where you need to record issues that are emerging from business operations. The programme manager manages this.
Monitoring and control strategy	Defines how the programme will apply internal controls to itself	The strategy is principally focused on how the control of the projects will be delivered. As their primary customer you must be comfortable that it will work. The programme manager creates this.
Organization structure	Description of the management roles, responsibilities and reporting lines in the programme	This document sets out the organization structure for the programme, and should include detail of your business change team, including your and their responsibilities and reporting lines. The programme manager creates this.
Programme brief	Used to assess whether the programme is viable and achievable	This includes a first draft of your benefits and outcomes, so it is very important in gaining support for moving the programme forward.
Programme communications plan	Sets out the timetable and arrangements for implementing and managing the stakeholder engagement strategy	It is likely that you and the other business change managers will be at the heart of the communications activities so will be heavily involved in creating and delivering this document. The programme manager creates this.
Programme definition document	A document that is used to consolidate or summarize the information that was used to define the programme	This is a document that defines what the programme will deliver. It could be used in place of the individual documents in the 'boundary' baseline. Your blueprint and benefits will appear in here if it is used. The programme manager creates this.

Title	Purpose	Why is it important to you?
Programme mandate	Used to describe the required outcomes from the programme, based on strategic or policy objectives	This document kicks the programme off and you will use it to develop the risks, benefits and major outcomes for the programme brief. It is provided to the programme, so it exists when the programme begins.
Programme plan	Used to control and track the progress and delivery of the programme and resulting outcomes	This document sets out what and when the programme will deliver. It can include a number of different plans such as the benefits realization plan. Therefore you will need to ensure you sign off the contents. The programme manager creates this.
Programme preparation plan	A plan that details how Defining a Programme will be undertaken	This is created at the end of Identifying a Programme stage and sets out how Defining a Programme will be delivered. You will be heavily involved in constructing the blueprint and the benefits, so you will be providing significant input to this. The programme manager creates this.
Projects dossier	Provides a list of the projects required to deliver the blueprint, with high-level information and estimates	This document summarizes all the projects that will be required and scopes each one to show how the blueprint will be delivered. So you are a customer for most of these projects. The programme manager creates this.
Quality and assurance plan	Sets out the timetable and arrangements for carrying out the quality and assurance strategy	This is the plan to implement the quality and assurance strategy. Ensure that it includes benefit and operational assurance reviews. The programme manager creates this.
Quality and assurance strategy	Used to define and establish the activities for managing quality across the programme	This document sets out how the programme will ensure there is adequate assurance and that it operates to an acceptable level of quality. Some of the quality areas are your responsibility so you need to be happy with the content and ensure assurance of operational readiness is undertaken. The programme manager creates this.
Resource management plan	Arrangements for implementing the resource management strategy	This is the schedule for deploying the resources and should include when your business change team will form and evolve. The programme manager creates this.

Table continues

Table A.2 *continued*

Title	Purpose	Why is it important to you?
Resource management strategy	Used to identify how the programme will acquire and manage the resources required to achieve the business change	This document sets out how the programme will be resourced, both in terms of projects and the business change team, so it should include your approach. The programme manager creates this.
Risk management strategy	Defines the programme approach to risk management	This sets out the framework for risks and the supporting process. You need to check that it doesn't conflict with other risk processes and that it is broad enough to meet your needs for handling operational and change-related risks. The programme manager creates this.
Risk register	Used to capture and actively manage the risks to the programme	This contains all the programme risks. Ensure that it has a categorization that enables you to monitor your operational and change risks. The programme manager creates this.
Stakeholder engagement strategy	Used to define the framework that will enable effective stakeholder engagement and communication	Sets out how stakeholders and communications will function, which is a key part of your role so you will need to contribute to the creation of this document and use any existing approaches. The programme manager creates this.
Stakeholder profiles	Used to record stakeholder analysis information	As you will be aware of what is happening throughout the organization you should be providing the information for the profiles to be created and updated. The programme manager creates this.
Vision statement	Used to communicate the end goal of the programme: could be seen as providing an external 'artist's impression' of the desired future state	This is the first document created as part of the programme brief so it will be part of your first job as the business change manager to help to create it. Ensure you buy into the vision and can sell it to your peers. The senior responsible owner creates this.

References

References

Association for Project Management (2012). *APM Body of Knowledge* (6th edition). See www.apm.org.uk

Bradley, Gerald (2010). *Fundamentals of Benefit Realization*. The Stationery Office, London.

Cabinet Office (2011). *Managing Successful Programmes*. The Stationery Office, London.

Jenner, Steve (2012). *Managing Benefits*. APMG-International.

Lean project management is an approach developed to deliver more with fewer resources. See, for example, www.lean.org

Myers–Briggs Type Indicator (MBTI®) assessment. See www.myersbriggs.org

Office of Government Commerce (2009). *Managing Successful Projects with PRINCE2*. The Stationery Office, London.

Project Management Institute (2012). *A Guide to the Project Management Institute Body of Knowledge (PMBOK® Guide)* (5th edition). See www.pmi.org

Six Sigma is an approach to improving the quality of process outputs by identifying and removing defects. See, for example, ISO 13053-1:2011

Smythe, John (2008). *The CEO: Chief Engagement Officer: Turning Hierarchy Upside Down to Drive Performance*. Gower, London.

The Open Group (2011). *TOGAF Version 9.1*. The Open Group Architecture Framework (TOGAF) is a framework for enterprise architecture. See www.opengroup.org

The Colour Works personality analysis tools. See www.thecolourworks.com

Index

Index